RV COOKING MADE EASY

RV
100 SIMPLE RECIPES FOR YOUR KITCHEN ON WHEELS
COOKING
MADE
EASY

HEATHER SCHLUETER

STERLING EPICURE
New York

STERLING EPICURE
New York

An Imprint of Sterling Publishing Co., Inc.

ISBN 978-1-4549-4429-4
ISBN 978-1-4549-4430-0 (e-book)

Distributed in Canada by Sterling Publishing Co., Inc.
c/o Canadian Manda Group, 664 Annette Street
Toronto, Ontario M6S 2C8, Canada
Distributed in the United Kingdom by GMC Distribution Services
Castle Place, 166 High Street, Lewes, East Sussex BN7 1XU, England
Distributed in Australia by NewSouth Books
University of New South Wales, Sydney, NSW 2052, Australia

For information about custom editions, special sales, and premium and corporate purchases, please contact Sterling Special Sales at 800-805-5489 or specialsales@sterlingpublishing.com.

Manufactured in China
2 4 6 8 10 9 7 5 3 1
sterlingpublishing.com

Cover design by Elizabeth Lindy
Interior design by Shannon Nicole Plunkett

Photo credits on page 200

To Bill and Elma Bernert,
who provided the inspiration
and knowledge that lit the
camping fire in our souls.
It all started with you.

CONTENTS

INTRODUCTION — 1

MEAL PLANNING & PREP — 5

   MEAL PLAN TEMPLATE — 12

BREAKFAST — 23

LUNCH & SNACKS — 53

DINNER — 90

SALADS & SIDES — 142

DESSERTS — 163

DRINKS — 181

CONVERSION CHARTS — 192

ABOUT THE AUTHOR — 193

INDEX — 194

PHOTO CREDITS — 200

INTRODUCTION

Twenty-five years ago, I used to send my kids to my sister and brother-in-law for a week, and they would take them camping along with their own kids. I had no interest. Send me to a five-star resort, please. And my kids would come back home every year full of stories and laughs and family bonding that would last a lifetime.

One year, my brother-in-law couldn't go, and my sister begged me to go instead. Let's just say it was not an easy task for her to convince me. But she did. So the two of us took our young children up to the pine tree–laden forest of northern Arizona in their little pop-up camper that could sleep an amazing number of people.

Getting there and setting up was a bit chaotic, to say the least. But the next morning, I woke before anyone, snuck out of the pop-up, started a morning fire, heated up a cup of joe, and sat there, curled up in my camp chair as I watched the sun sneak up over the horizon to stream through those pines, creating the most spectacular and peaceful scenery I had ever seen. I was hooked.

After that trip, I went home and bought my very first camper—a small pop-up just like my sister's. And we've been camping ever since. I've had everything from that little pop-up to a forty-foot Class A motor home to a tow-behind pod with an outdoor kitchen to a thirty-six-foot fifth wheel. I love them all and I could happily camp today in any of these RVs. It's all about the experience.

And food is a huge part of the experience. I don't recall what I made on that inaugural trip (hot dogs and Pop-Tarts® ring a bell) but I have now cooked in every type of RV out there for the past twenty-five years. In fact, our families still go RVing together, and I do all the food planning and cooking for our trips. It makes me happy (and it makes my sister happy, too!).

My goal with this book is to bring together everything I've learned about RV cooking over twenty-five years and share the tips, tricks, and recipes that have always worked so that you can spend less time stressing about food and more time enjoying your own RV experience—creating memories, stories, laughs, and life-long bonds.

Give me the choice today between RVing and a five-star resort, and RVing wins. Every. Single. Time.

PANTRY STAPLES AND ORGANIZATION

Storage space. Countertop space. Refrigerator space. All are in short supply in an RV and can cause cooking challenges. But with some careful planning and organization, you can put together an amazing variety of fabulous meals, even while you're out enjoying quality family time in the great outdoors.

Each recipe in this book has its own set of ingredients, but the following is a list of general good-to-have-around seasonings and staples. Keep the size of your kitchen in mind when selecting ingredients. If you have a tiny kitchen with a very tiny pantry, salt, pepper, and Italian seasoning will go a very long way.

SPICES

Salt	Grilling spice blend	Dried basil
Black pepper	Garlic powder	Dried oregano
Italian seasoning	Onion powder	Dried thyme
Seasoned salt	Ground cinnamon	Dried rosemary
Cayenne pepper	Red pepper flakes	

OILS/CONDIMENTS/SAUCES

Olive oil
(regular & extra-virgin)

Nonstick cooking spray

White wine vinegar

Balsamic vinegar

Tabasco

Soy sauce

Hoisin sauce

Maple syrup

Relish

Mustard

Steak sauce

BBQ sauce

PANTRY STAPLES

All-purpose flour

White sugar

Brown sugar

Cornstarch

Baking powder

Coffee & coffee creamer

Breadcrumbs
(regular & panko)

Pantry organization is essential in an RV kitchen due to the limited space, and I have tried any number of solutions to keep things neat and tidy. Typically, RV cupboards tend to be deep to utilize all available space. But this can make it difficult to see or reach items in the back of the cupboard, and it's rare to find a good, confined space to keep spice jars and bottles.

Here's how I make the most of my RV kitchen:

1. Use small plastic bins that fit into smaller kitchen cabinets to store spice jars. These bins will typically fit in the upper small cabinets. Organize the spices alphabetically so each one is easy to find when you need it.

2. Use a larger plastic bin for liquids such as oils, vinegars, and syrup. Keeping them all in one container will limit any potential

mess, should one of the containers get jostled around and tip over (yes, that happens!).

3. Keep breads in an open cubby, if possible, to reduce the potential for mold. Flat breads, such as pita or tortillas, take up far less space and usually last longer than regular loaf bread.

4. Put baking staples such as flour and sugar in sturdy plastic containers with lids. Empty plastic nut containers from warehouse stores work well and can usually be stacked neatly on top of each other without creating a mess.

5. Put taller, boxed items such as cereal, crackers, and cookies in the back of larger cabinets. They will be easy to see and easy to reach.

6. Keep canned goods together and in front of boxed items but be mindful of the weight. Some RV shelving is a little weak and can easily be overloaded, causing them to bow.

7. Place bags of chips and items that are frequently grabbed in an easy-to-reach but high cabinet.

8. Due to the weight, bottled water should be placed in cabinets on the floor.

MEAL PLANNING
& PREP

Proper meal planning can make the difference between a relaxing and enjoyable experience with family and friends or a stressful and miserable RV trip. I love cooking in the great outdoors—whether I'm outside using a portable grill or camp oven, or in the RV using the cooktop or oven.

No matter how you intend to prepare meals, everything is easier and goes more smoothly with some solid menu planning. It gives you more time to enjoy the beautiful scenery around you, as well as those who are traveling with you. It's well worth the beforehand effort.

My family does everything from weekend warrior trips to multi-week getaways (and we look forward to full-timing it!). No matter the length of the trip, I always plan the meals and do a fair amount of food prep in advance. Over the years, I've developed a system that works well. Here are the keys to successful RV meal planning and prep:

Get an accurate head count of how many mouths you will have to feed for any given meal—This number can change throughout the trip, depending on others who may join you at various times.

Take note of any food aversions or allergies that your fellow RVers may have—With limited storage space, it can be difficult to make separate meals for those with food issues, so it's best to know what they are in advance.

Plan to use fresh ingredients first to avoid spoilage—Leafy lettuces, ripe tomatoes, strawberries, and bananas are items that tend to spoil quickly, so put those items at the beginning of the menu.

Plan meals on back-to-back days, when you're using only half of the same ingredient for each meal—For example: BLT Sandwiches (page 59) and Frozen Hamburgers Done Right (page 72) should be made on back-to-back days, because you'll use about half of the head of lettuce for each meal. This method allows for all of the lettuce to be consumed, rather than half of it spoiling and needing to be tossed.

Mix up the menu with items you can make ahead and those that can be made at the campsite—Plan to serve make-ahead meals to heat and eat on days when you're busy or tired. If you change location or go day tripping, hiking, or exploring, you'll want a fast meal for everyone.

Try to keep leftovers to a minimum—Filling your RV fridge with multiple containers of half portions of meals takes up more space than you have. However, if a recipe gives you two full meals' worth of food, then absolutely keep those leftovers. You'll enjoy them on a day when you want to relax.

Prep some ingredients beforehand to save space in the RV refrigerator—Dicing onions, scrambling eggs, leafing lettuce, and chopping broccoli into florets in advance will save tons of room in the fridge. Determine which of these space-saving tips will help once you've planned the full menu.

Here are a couple of sample meal plans, one for a long weekend and another to cover meals for two weeks. You can change them up, depending on your personal tastes, or use the template on page 8 to make your own meal plan.

LONG WEEKEND MEAL PLAN

THURSDAY (NUMBER = NUMBER OF PEOPLE)

Breakfast (2) — Vanilla Cream Steel Cut Oatmeal with Berries (page 51)

Lunch (2) — Charcuterie Board (page 56)

Snack (2) — Fresh fruit

Dinner (2) — Grilled Chicken Quesadillas (page 134)

Dessert (2) — Grilled Glazed Pineapple Spears (page 180)

FRIDAY

Breakfast (4) — Make-Ahead Breakfast "Quiche" (page 32)

Lunch (4) — Frozen Hamburgers Done Right (page 72)

Snack (4) — Basic Hard-Boiled Eggs (page 52)

Dinner (4) — Caprese Chicken (page 112)

Dessert (4) — Peanut Butter Chocolate Banana Boat (page 179)

SATURDAY

Breakfast (4) — Perfect Scrambled Eggs (page 36),
Oven-Baked Bacon (page 43), and Toast (page 26)

Lunch (4) — BLT Sandwiches (page 59)

Snack (4) — No-Bake Protein Balls (page 55)

Dinner (4) — Hawaiian Chicken Skewers (page 71) and Foil Packet Broccoli
on the Grill (page 155)

Dessert (4) — S'mores Bake (page 177)

SUNDAY

Breakfast (4) — Make-Ahead Breakfast Burritos (page 28)

Lunch (2) — Shredded Chicken Gyros (page 84)

Snack (2) — Fresh fruit

Dinner (2) — Meatloaf Muffins (page 93) and Grilled Corn on the Cob (page 161)

Dessert (2) — Mini Cherry Pies (page 172)

TWO-WEEK MEAL PLAN

A note about the two-week plan: I planned on four people for all meals. Adjust as necessary for your group. We generally eat breakfast before we hit the road on the first day of any trip, so I didn't include it in the plan.

FRIDAY

Lunch/Snack — Fruit and chips

Dinner/Dessert — Grilled Chicken Quesadillas (page 134) and Apple Pie Packets (page 170)

SATURDAY

Breakfast — Breakfast Scramble (page 37) with tortillas

Lunch/Snack — Baked Brats with Onions and Peppers (page 67)

Dinner/Dessert — Beef and Tomato Skewers (page 79) and Simple Chopped Green Salad (page 144)

SUNDAY

Breakfast — Vanilla Cream Steel Cut Oatmeal with Berries (page 51)

Lunch/Snack — Frozen Hamburgers Done Right (page 72)

Dinner/Dessert — Loaded Baked Potato Casserole (page 96) and S'mores Bake (page 177)

MONDAY

Breakfast — Make-Ahead Breakfast Burritos (page 28)

Lunch/Snack — Charcuterie Board (page 56)

Dinner/Dessert — Grilled Boneless Pork Chops (page 131) and Cucumber Tomato Salad (page 145)

TUESDAY

Breakfast — Perfect Scrambled Eggs (page 36),
Oven-Baked Bacon (page 43), and Toast (page 26)

Lunch/Snack — Carolina-Style BBQ Chicken Sandwiches (page 86)
and Easy Coleslaw (page 143)

Dinner/Dessert — Beef Enchilada Bake (page 91)
and Skillet Cake and Berries (page 166)

WEDNESDAY

Breakfast — Yogurt and Berry Parfait (page 25)

Lunch/Snack — Shredded Chicken Gyros (page 84)

Dinner/Dessert — Easy BBQ Meatball Skewers (page 138)
and Spinach Salad with Strawberries (page 146)

THURSDAY

Breakfast — Make-Ahead Pressure Cooker Egg Bites (page 34)

Lunch/Snack — Quick Philly Cheesesteak Sandwiches (page 80) and fresh fruit

Dinner/Dessert — Chicken, Potato, and Broccoli Foil Packets (page 126) and
Mini Cherry Pies (page 172)

FRIDAY

Breakfast — French Toast (page 41)

Lunch/Snack — Sloppy Joes (page 62) and Easy Coleslaw (page 143)

Dinner/Dessert — One-Pot Spaghetti (page 107)

SATURDAY

Breakfast — Make-Ahead Egg Muffin Sandwiches (page 30)

Lunch/Snack — Grilled Chicken Tender Sandwiches (page 74) and Grilled Corn
on the Cob (page 161)

Dinner/Dessert — Grilled Flank Steak (page 132), Grilled Vegetable Salad (page 158),
and Blueberry Crumble (page 174)

SUNDAY

Breakfast — Vanilla Cream Steel Cut Oatmeal with Berries (page 51)

Lunch/Snack — Ham Rolls (page 58) and chips

Dinner/Dessert — Sweet and Sour Pork Packets (page 128)
and Cherry Chocolate Cake (page 173)

MONDAY

Breakfast — Tater Tot™ Breakfast Casserole (page 48)

Lunch/Snack — Pulled Pork Pizza (page 88)

Dinner/Dessert — Stuffed Baked Potatoes (page 114)
and Mini Cherry Pies (page 172)

TUESDAY

Breakfast — Make-Ahead Breakfast Burritos (page 28)

Lunch/Snack — Shredded Chicken Tacos (page 60)

Dinner/Dessert — Grilled BBQ Chicken Drumsticks and Thighs (page 76),
Grilled Zucchini (page 157), and Herbed Baby Potatoes (page 151)

WEDNESDAY

Breakfast — Sheet Pan Chicken and Waffles (page 46)

Lunch/Snack — Chili Cheese Dogs (page 75)

Dinner/Dessert — Orzo and Chicken Medley (page 104)
and Grilled Glazed Pineapple Spears (page 180)

THURSDAY

Breakfast — Make-Ahead Breakfast "Quiche" (page 32)

Lunch/Snack — Turkey Lettuce Wraps (page 66)

Dinner/Dessert — Shepherd's Pie, Thanksgiving Style (page 98)
and No-Bake Mini Cheesecakes (page 164)

ONE-WEEK MEAL PLAN TEMPLATE

We generally eat breakfast before we leave on Day 1, so I don't include it in the plan. Insert the number of people in the parentheses.

DAY 1 _____

  Lunch/Snack [   ] _____

_____

  Dinner/Dessert [   ] _____

_____

DAY 2 _____

  Breakfast [   ] _____

  Lunch/Snack [   ] _____

_____

  Dinner/Dessert [   ] _____

_____

DAY 3 _____

  Breakfast [   ] _____

  Lunch/Snack [   ] _____

_____

  Dinner/Dessert [   ] _____

_____

DAY 4 _____

    Breakfast [ ] _____

    Lunch/Snack [ ] _____

    _____

    Dinner/Dessert [ ] _____

    _____

DAY 5 _____

    Breakfast [ ] _____

    Lunch/Snack [ ] _____

    _____

    Dinner/Dessert [ ] _____

    _____

DAY 6 _____

    Breakfast [ ] _____

    Lunch/Snack [ ] _____

    _____

    Dinner/Dessert [ ] _____

    _____

NOTES: _____

_____

DAY 7 _____

   Breakfast [   ] _____

   Lunch/Snack [   ] _____

   _____

   Dinner/Dessert [   ] _____

   _____

NOTES: _____

_____

_____

Resource Management

RV travel brings freedom. Freedom to pick up and go whenever and wherever the mood strikes. Freedom to see all that this beautiful country has to offer. Freedom to meet up with family and friends to create lifelong memories.

But RV travel also has some restrictions. Power, storage space, refrigerator and freezer dimensions, and water all may be in limited supply. When managed properly, however, the limitations will hardly create a blip in your plans.

POWER CONSIDERATIONS

Let's face it—your RV needs power. Lights, electronics, heaters, and especially kitchen appliances consume a lot of power. It is imperative to know and understand your own RV's power capabilities, particularly when camping off-grid or in the wild, also called boondocking.

RVs can have everything from a single house battery, which must support all systems, to a very sophisticated multibattery solar system with inverters and controllers that can handle even the largest power loads. Learn what your RV has and stay well within its capabilities and you'll be just fine.

Even when plugged into shore power—when you're connected to the AC electric grid—RVs still may have limitations. Are you plugged into 110 volts? Or 30 or 50 amps?

The answers to those questions will determine which kitchen appliances are appropriate for your RV. When our solar-powered system was installed, the technician asked us the importance of each kitchen appliance in descending order so he could determine exactly how much power we needed when boondocking. This is a great exercise for anyone with an RV and will help you decide which appliances are "must-haves" and which ones can stay home.

For me, easy morning coffee is essential (although I do love a good pour-over coffee on occasion). One round of toast in a toaster is pretty high on the list, as well as the use of my three-quart electric pressure cooker, but regular use of a microwave is not at all important to me.

Even though the solar power in our RV was built to meet our family's needs, I keep in mind roughly how much power each appliance uses whenever I plug it in, so I don't overload the power source that is supporting us. Here are some common small kitchen appliances and their average wattages to help you decide which ones are essential to you.

Drip coffee maker	750 watts
Keurig® coffee maker	1,500 watts (peak usage)
Two-slice toaster	1,000 watts
Toaster oven	1,400 watts
Three-quart pressure cooker	700 watts
Six-quart pressure cooker	1,100 watts
Microwave	1,200 watts
Hand mixer	250 watts
Blender	1,000 watts (average)
Waffle iron	1,000 watts
Sous vide circulator*	1,000 watts

*Note: this is one of my favorite appliances, but repeated high and low cycling makes it a poor choice for battery draw, so sadly, this one stays home when we might be boondocking.

Storage Considerations

The last consideration for kitchen appliances is storage—always in short supply. We have a decent amount of countertop space, so our toaster and coffee maker can stay on the counter, but the pressure cooker and blender have to be stored when not in use. In the end, lack of space, rather than power consumption, may ultimately determine which appliances go with you on your RV adventures.

Refrigerator/Freezer Considerations

Keeping things cool seems like such a simple topic, doesn't it? But it may be one of the most complicated resource management tasks to get right. And it is potentially one of the most important. ('Cause who wants warm beer?)

RV refrigerators and freezers tend to be less efficient than residential units. They take longer to cool down, have a harder time keeping up with an influx of warm food and drinks, and often struggle to freeze ice. But with a little extra thought and care, your RV fridge and freezer will keep you happy.

Arizona is my family's home base, so we must turn on our refrigerator to cool it down at least twenty-four to forty-eight hours before loading the food. If it is very hot outside, I will also put a "sacrificial" bag of ice in the freezer, which helps draw cooler air into the main refrigerator space. That bag of ice will often partially or fully melt, but it's well worth it to make sure the entire refrigerator and freezer are cool and ready for food.

When the refrigerator is cooled down, I load up any premade frozen food, like Loaded Baked Potato Casserole (page 96). I stack frozen casseroles on top of each other and fill in the other spaces with items like frozen vegetables or frozen burgers. A freezer can be tightly packed without negatively affecting its performance.

The refrigerator is a different story. It needs lots of cool airflow to remain efficient and fully functional. Do not overpack your refrigerator. (Let me repeat . . . do not stuff the fridge!) An over-packed refrigerator results in freezing some foods while leaving others at temperatures that are not safe to eat, causing premature spoilage. (Okay, lecture is over . . .)

When packing both the refrigerator and freezer, it is a very good idea to precool or prefreeze items in your regular residential refrigerator first. This prevents your RV fridge from working too hard. When this is not possible, put only a few uncooled items in the RV refrigerator at a time to make sure other items do not warm up.

ICE

There's nothing like an ice-cold beverage at a campground—especially that first one—right when you pull in. But perfectly chilled drinks don't just happen by themselves. Ice plays a big role.

Ice is easy to come by much of the time, but not so much when you're boondocking, at a music festival, or in some small towns where the price of ice may be a little up there. So this section is to help you with ice management.

Space in the RV freezer is usually limited, so throwing in a full bag of ice will take up some much-needed room for all of that wonderful premade and frozen food you've prepared. Plus, it's easy to plow through those bags of ice when you're making mixed drinks. So what's the solution?

Large ice cubes. I'm talking about making ice beforehand, using silicone trays that produce six to eight large ice cubes (usually about 2 x 2 inches each). There are two reasons why I love this method. The first is the space-saving aspect—I make anywhere from thirty-two to ninety-six jumbo ice cubes (depending on the length of the trip) before we leave. One gallon-size resealable bag will easily hold sixteen ice cubes—and it lies flat. I make enough ice cubes for two to six gallon bags. The bags, which lie flat on top of each other, are stacked in our RV freezer. This arrangement takes up far less room than even one regular store-bought bag of ice.

The other reason why I love big ice cubes (and I'm gonna get a little scientific on you . . .) is that they melt more slowly than smaller cubes of the same volume. Why is that? It has to do with surface area. The rate of ice melt is directly proportional to the amount of surface area of the ice that is exposed to the liquid in which it sits—the more surface area, the more the ice crystals transfer to the warmer liquid. The volume of ice in one large chunk has less surface area than the same volume of ice in multiple small ice cubes. And when ice melts more slowly, your drink doesn't get watered down. There you have it! Large ice cubes for the win!

COOLERS

There are as many opinions about coolers as there are coolers to buy. Big? Small? Portable? Expensive? Bargain brand? So, what *is* the perfect cooler to take RVing? Well, the answer isn't simple. It really depends on your personal needs.

In the discussion about ice and ice management, above, I favored making large ice cubes for packing into your RV freezer. But that's not always possible, and you may need bagged ice because of space constraints, or perhaps you're going on a long trip. In that case, I suggest investing in a high-quality cooler with thick sides and a tight seal.

I have used many name-brand, upper-end coolers (Yeti®, Pelican™, Orion, etc.) and I believe they all perform equally well. The best way to utilize these higher-priced coolers is to pack them full with bags of ice (not drinks). And open the cooler only when it's absolutely necessary. This will keep the ice bags rock solid for days.

So what about drinks? To keep them nicely chilled, it's okay to use a lower-priced cooler. Put your drinks (prechilled if possible) into the cooler and top the containers with lots of fresh ice. And open the cooler only when necessary, just as you would with a higher-end model (and please don't stand there with the lid open, just daydreaming about what you want. Think about what you want and then open the lid quickly, retrieve what you're looking for, and then close the lid just as quickly). I know this may sound a little extreme, but if you really want super-cold beverages, this is hands-down the best way to manage your cooler without constantly having to buy more ice.

We also have a soft-sided, small cooler that we use on day trips for snacks and drinks. These coolers typically come with a reusable ice pack that can be frozen again after use. These handy coolers are collapsible when not in use, and take up little space.

As I've mentioned, the type, size, and number of coolers you use is a personal preference, but my cooler system has worked well for many years, and I recommend giving it a try.

WATER CONSIDERATIONS

Water can be a real issue when RVing. And water management is critical to a successful RV trip. It is necessary not only for cooking and cleaning, but also for the health and survival of all those along for the adventure.

Most of my RV experience has been in the Southwest, where it's hot and dry, so water usage and consumption take on a whole new meaning, and water conservation is essential. Here are some of the water tips and tricks I have developed throughout the years. Keep these tips in mind and you'll never run into water issues.

- Always have plenty of extra drinking water on hand, regardless of whether there will be water available at your campsite. I bring several one-gallon water jugs (can be reusable) on each outing.

- Determine whether the campsite you are going to has potable (drinkable) water, and if it can be deposited in your RV water tank. Many places have non-threaded spigots that are deliberately designed to prevent RVers from filling their RV water tanks. We ran into this many times in Colorado. Be aware ahead of time and arrive with a full tank of water, if necessary.

- Install a water filter on your RV water system. It can be attached directly to your kitchen sink or where the water feeds the entire RV from the main water tank. These tanks can be very dirty, and you want to prevent that dirt from clogging up your water system.

- In general, we travel with our RV water tank empty to save on fuel consumption while driving, but we always fill the tank first if we are going to a place where we might not have access to fresh water.

- When cleaning dishes, keep the water flow from the kitchen sink to a trickle, or use a bin filled with soapy water to wash dishes and then lightly rinse them.

- Coffee uses a lot of water. Plan accordingly.

- Always keep an eye on the amount of water you have in the water tank and have a plan to refill it long before you run out.

BREAKFAST

Yogurt and Berry Parfait

Creamy vanilla yogurt, crunchy granola, and cool berries all come together in this super-easy, no-cook breakfast. It's perfect when you want something light to get your day going.

1. Spoon 4 ounces of the yogurt into the bottom of each of 4 tall glasses or disposable cups. Add ¼ cup of the berries on top of the yogurt in each glass or cup, then add ¼ cup of granola on top of the berries. Repeat the layers; there will be a total of six layers in each glass.

2. Refrigerate or serve immediately.

YIELD: 4 SERVINGS

PREP TIME: 5 minutes

COOKING TIME: 0 minutes

1 (32-ounce) container vanilla yogurt

2 cups fresh or frozen berries, thawed

2 cups granola of choice

Toast—Four Options

Okay, I get it. It's only toast. But sometimes getting great toast in an RV (especially when boondocking) can be a real challenge. So here are my top four ways to get perfect toast for breakfast.

USING A TOASTER

1. Use when on shore power or if you have sufficient solar power.

2. Place bread slices in the toaster and toast according to toaster instructions.

3. When toasted, smear each slice with ½ tablespoon of butter and serve.

USING A TOASTER OVEN

1. Use only when on shore power.

2. Place 4 slices of bread on a baking sheet and toast according to toaster oven instructions.

3. When toasted, smear each slice with ½ tablespoon of butter and serve.

YIELD: 4 SLICES

PREP TIME: 1 minute

COOKING TIME: 4 minutes

4 slices bread

2 tablespoons butter

USING A PORTABLE STAND-UP TOASTER RACK

1. Use when boondocking or when you don't want to use electric power.

2. Place the toaster rack directly on the propane cooktop and arrange 4 pieces of bread vertically on the rack.

3. Turn heat to medium-high. Toast approximately 3 minutes, and then turn the bread to the other side and toast another 3 minutes, or to your preferred doneness.

4. When toasted, smear each slice with ½ tablespoon of butter and serve.

USING A BROILER

1. Use when boondocking or don't want to use electric power.

2. Turn the broiler on.

3. Place 4 slices of bread on a baking sheet.

4. Place the baking sheet under the broiler for 2 to 3 minutes, and then turn the bread over to toast the other side for another 2 to 3 minutes. Check frequently to make sure the bread doesn't burn.

5. When toasted, smear each slice with ½ tablespoon of butter and serve.

Make-Ahead Breakfast Burritos

Loaded with all the breakfast flavor you could want, these burritos have been a staple for over a decade on our RV travels. I make and freeze them before every trip and pull them out on "move days" to make the morning easier.

1. Make Tater Tots according to package directions, if using.

2. In a large nonstick skillet, cook the sausage until crumbly and fully cooked. Remove the cooked sausage and set aside.

3. In the same pan, scramble the eggs, then add salsa at the end and fully combine.

4. In a large bowl, combine egg and salsa mixture, cheese, and sausage. Mix together. Fold in the cooked Tater Tots, if using.

5. Divide the mixture equally among the eight tortillas. Fold in one end of each tortilla, then roll the tortilla around the filling to close.

6. Lightly coat eight pieces of aluminum foil with the cooking spray.

 Make Ahead

YIELD: 8 BURRITOS

PREP TIME: 5 minutes
COOKING TIME: 15 minutes
REHEAT TIME: 20 minutes

2 cups frozen Tater Tots (optional)

1 pound ground sausage (I prefer spicy Italian)

12 eggs

½ cup salsa

2 cups shredded cheese, Mexican blend

8 flour tortillas, burrito size

Nonstick cooking spray

7. Snugly wrap each burrito in the sprayed foil, cool for 15 minutes, then freeze for up to 3 months.

8. Move the burritos from the freezer to the refrigerator the day before serving.

9. When serving, preheat the oven or camp grill to 325°F. Heat the burritos in the foil for 20 minutes, or until heated through.

Make-Ahead Egg Muffin Sandwiches

These breakfast sandwiches are so much better than the fast-food version and they're a cinch to make before any camping trip. Just wrap them individually in foil, then pop them into your RV oven to warm them up when you're ready for an easy morning meal.

1. In a medium bowl, beat the eggs and then add the salt and pepper.

2. Heat a medium skillet over medium-high heat and add the oil. Pour the eggs into the skillet and let them sit 1 to 2 minutes, until they begin to cook around the edges. Lightly stir to cook the eggs another 5 minutes, or until the eggs are cooked all the way through. Take the skillet off the heat and let the eggs sit undisturbed.

3. Toast the English muffins.

4. Butter one side of the muffins, then place one quarter of the egg mixture onto each muffin. Top with one slice each of ham and cheese, and top with the other half of the muffin. Tightly wrap each assembled muffin in foil. Cool for 15 minutes and then freeze for up to 3 months.

 Make Ahead

YIELD: 4 SERVINGS

PREP TIME: 5 minutes
COOKING TIME: 10 minutes
REHEAT TIME: 20 minutes

6 eggs
½ teaspoon salt
¼ teaspoon pepper
1 tablespoon olive oil
4 English muffins
2 tablespoons butter
4 slices deli ham
4 slices American cheese

5. Move the muffins from the freezer to the refrigerator the evening before serving.

6. To serve, preheat the oven to 350°F and bake the wrapped muffins for 20 minutes, or until heated through.

Make-Ahead Breakfast "Quiche"

This may be the meal that started it all. My sister's in-laws are the instigators of our entire family's camping obsession, and we meet up with them multiple times a year. This delicious "quiche" is her Sunday morning tradition, and we all look forward to it. Thank you, Elma, for all the wonderful Sunday-morning memories. Many more to come!

1. Preheat the oven to 425°F and, with the nonstick cooking spray, lightly coat a disposable aluminum 9 x 13-inch pan (be sure the pan fits in your RV oven).

2. Press the thawed potatoes O'Brien into the bottom and 1 inch up the side of the pan, making a "crust," and sprinkle with seasoned salt. Bake for 25 minutes.

3. While the potatoes are baking, in a medium skillet, brown the sausage over medium-high heat for 6 minutes, or until the sausage is fully cooked and crumbled. Drain the fat. Return the sausage to the skillet.

4. Remove the potatoes from the oven after 25 minutes and reduce the oven temperature to 350°F.

 Make Ahead

YIELD: 8 SERVINGS

PREP TIME: 5 minutes

COOKING TIME: 55 minutes

REHEAT TIME: 30 to 45 minutes

Nonstick cooking spray

1 (28-ounce) bag frozen potatoes O'Brien (with peppers and onions), thawed

½ teaspoon seasoned salt

1 pound ground hot Italian sausage

1 cup shredded Monterey Jack cheese

1 cup shredded Swiss cheese

1½ cups half-and-half

6 eggs

5. Quickly toss the sausage and cheeses together in the skillet, then spread the mixture on top of the potatoes.

6. In a medium bowl, beat together the half-and-half and the eggs, then pour the mixture over the sausage and potatoes in the pan.

7. Bake the quiche, uncovered, for 30 minutes and then remove it from the oven. Let the quiche come to room temperature and then cover it tightly with foil and freeze for up to 3 months.

8. Remove the quiche from the freezer and place it in the refrigerator 2 days before serving. Remove the quiche from the refrigerator 30 minutes before reheating. Preheat the oven to 350°F. Bake the quiche, covered, for 30 to 45 minutes, to warm through. Remove the foil for the last 10 minutes. Serve immediately.

Make-Ahead Pressure Cooker Egg Bites

These egg bites were made famous by Starbucks, but they can easily be made with a silicone egg tray in a pressure cooker, or in your home or RV oven. It's really worth it to use Gruyère cheese, but Swiss will do in a pinch. I make a batch of egg bites before we hit the road, so I always have a quick and easy heat-and-eat breakfast ready to go. There are lots of topping options for the eggs, too, so have fun with them!

1. Put eggs, cheeses, salt, and pepper into a blender and blend for 30 seconds.

2. Spray the silicone egg tray with nonstick cooking spray and fill each well three-quarters full with the egg mixture. (If you're using an oven, pour the mixture into greased muffin tins and bake at 375°F for 30 minutes.)

3. Pour 1 cup of water into the pressure cooker inner pot and insert the trivet. Lower the filled egg tray onto the trivet. Cover with foil or a tray cover. Secure the lid and pressure cook on high pressure for 8 minutes, ensuring the pressure valve is in the sealing position.

4. When cook time is complete, let the pressure cooker naturally release (sit undisturbed) for 5 minutes, then

 Make Ahead

YIELD: 4 SERVINGS

PREP TIME: 10 minutes
COOKING TIME: 13 minutes
TOTAL TIME: 30 minutes
REHEAT TIME: 20 minutes

6 eggs

½ cup grated Gruyère cheese

¼ cup cottage cheese

¼ teaspoon salt

¼ teaspoon pepper

Nonstick cooking spray

ingredients continue on following page

move the pressure valve toward the venting position to quick-release the remaining pressure. Carefully remove the lid and remove the egg tray.

5. Using a spoon, remove the egg bites from the tray and invert them onto a plate. Top with grated Gruyere cheese, sprinkle of cayenne pepper, crumbled bacon, or green onions, depending on your taste.

6. Let the egg bites come to room temperature, then wrap them in foil, two bites per sheet of foil. Freeze for up to 3 months.

7. Transfer the egg bites from the freezer to the refrigerator the night before serving.

8. Preheat the oven to 350°F and place the thawed egg bites (still in foil) into the oven. Bake for 20 minutes, then serve.

TOPPINGS

2 tablespoons grated Gruyère cheese, optional

Sprinkle of cayenne pepper, optional

4 strips cooked bacon, crumbled (see Oven-Baked Bacon, page 43), optional

2 tablespoons minced green onions, optional

Perfect Scrambled Eggs

There really is a secret to fluffy, flavorful scrambled eggs. Just follow this recipe to a T and you'll savor every last bite of these perfect scrambled eggs.

1. Crack the eggs into a large bowl and add the milk, salt, and pepper. Beat the mixture until well blended.

2. Heat a large nonstick skillet over medium-high heat and add the butter.

3. When the butter has melted, pour the egg mixture into the pan. Using a silicone spatula, continually stir the eggs for 5 to 7 minutes, scraping the entire bottom of the skillet regularly until the eggs are just shy of the desired doneness.

4. When the eggs are slightly runny, turn off the heat from under the pan, but continue to stir the eggs with the spatula for another minute.

5. Transfer the eggs to plates or a serving platter as soon as they are cooked through. They should still be very moist and not dry or rubbery.

6. Serve with Toast (page 26) and Oven-Baked Bacon (page 43).

 Cooktop

YIELD: 4 SERVINGS

PREP TIME: 5 minutes
COOKING TIME: 10 minutes

10 eggs

¼ cup milk

1 teaspoon salt

½ teaspoon pepper

1 tablespoon butter

Breakfast Scramble

When you want to kick your scrambled eggs up a notch, this will do the trick. The addition of minced onion and ground sausage transforms simple scrambled eggs into a stick-to-your-ribs breakfast that will keep you satisfied all morning long.

1. Place a large skillet over high heat and add the butter and onion. Sauté the onion for 3 to 5 minutes, or until it softens.

2. Add the ground sausage and cook 5 to 7 minutes, until the meat is cooked through and crumbly.

3. In a bowl, lightly scramble the eggs with a fork, then add to the sausage mixture and stir continuously for 5 minutes, or until the eggs are nearly cooked through. A silicone spatula works well for this.

4. Add the cheese, if using, salt, and pepper and cook another 1 to 2 minutes until the eggs are cooked through.

5. Serve with a hot cup of coffee and a smile.

 Cooktop

YIELD: 4 SERVINGS

PREP TIME: 10 minutes
COOKING TIME: 15 minutes

1 tablespoon butter

½ medium onion, any kind, minced

½ pound ground sausage (I prefer hot Italian sausage)

8 eggs

¼ cup shredded cheese of choice (optional)

½ teaspoon salt

¼ teaspoon pepper

Classic Corned Beef Hash Breakfast

Crispy but tender corned beef hash is all about technique, and my husband has perfected it. The key is to leave that corned beef hash untouched for the first 10 minutes. No cheating! It works.

 Cooktop

YIELD: 4 SERVINGS

PREP TIME: 3 minutes

COOKING TIME: 15 minutes

1 (15-ounce) can corned beef hash

3 tablespoons water, plus more if needed

4 eggs

1. Place a large skillet over medium-high heat. Add the corned beef hash and spread it out, into a layer, approximately ½ inch thick. Let the hash sit in the skillet over medium-high heat for approximately 10 minutes, uncovered and undisturbed, until the bottom is crispy.

2. Using a spoon, push in some of the corned beef from the edge of the skillet (for the addition of water). Create four wells in the corned beef hash for the eggs. (The wells don't need to go all the way to the bottom of the pan; they should be just deep enough to keep the eggs from running everywhere). Crack an egg into each well.

3. Add 3 tablespoons of water to the area of the pan that has been cleared. Cover and reduce the heat to medium-low to poach the

eggs. Check the eggs after 2 minutes to see if they need more water. Add another tablespoon of water, if needed, to continue poaching the eggs for another 1 to 2 minutes to get the desired yolk. (After 3 minutes total, the eggs will be fairly runny; after 4 minutes they'll be firmer.) I like them a little runny.

4. Serve as soon as the eggs are done.

French Toast

It's amazing how easy it is to make this wonderfully decadent breakfast. And you can kick it up a notch by using fresh berries and a dollop of whipped cream as a topping.

1. In a large bowl, beat together the eggs, milk, cinnamon, and salt.

2. Place a large, nonstick skillet over medium-high heat and add the butter.

3. When the butter has melted, dip each slice of bread into the egg mixture, coating both sides. Let any excess egg mixture drain off the bread and then place the coated bread onto the hot, buttered pan. The pan will hold 2 to 4 slices.

4. Cook the bread undisturbed for 2 to 3 minutes, then flip and cook the other side for another 2 to 3 minutes. The outside should look cooked with spotty brown patches. Repeat until all 8 pieces are cooked.

5. Remove the bread to four plates and serve with syrup.

 Cooktop

YIELD: 4 SERVINGS

PREP TIME: 5 minutes

COOKING TIME: 10 minutes

4 eggs

¼ cup milk

1 teaspoon ground cinnamon

½ teaspoon salt

1 tablespoon butter

8 slices thick or regular sliced bread

Maple syrup for serving

Sausage Gravy and Biscuits

Rich, creamy, flavorful, and completely satisfying—biscuits and sausage gravy are a favorite among RVers, and for good reason. You'll love this easy version.

1. Bake the biscuits according to package directions.

2. Place a large skillet over high heat and add the butter. When the butter has melted, add the sausage and cook 8 to 10 minutes, or until the meat is crumbly and no longer pink.

3. Sprinkle the sausage with the flour and cook another minute, or until all the flour has been absorbed.

4. Slowly add the milk to the meat mixture, constantly whisking it in, and bring it to a boil. Reduce the heat and simmer 3 to 4 more minutes. Remove the skillet from the heat.

5. Split each biscuit and place one or two halves into a bowl (depending on how hungry you are!). Spoon the sausage gravy over the top and serve immediately.

Cooktop and oven

YIELD: 6 SERVINGS

PREP TIME: 10 minutes
COOKING TIME: 15 minutes

1 16-ounce tube refrigerated biscuits

2 tablespoons butter

1 pound ground sausage (hot, mild, or country, or maple flavored)

¼ cup all-purpose flour

3 cups whole or low-fat milk

Oven-Baked Bacon

Bacon. 'Nuff said. What's camping without bacon? Baking bacon is the easiest way to get perfect bacon without a big, greasy mess. Win-win.

1. Preheat the oven to 425°F. Line a rimmed baking sheet with aluminum foil.

2. Place all the bacon strips very close together, without overlapping, on the prepared baking sheet. Bake for 15 to 20 minutes, flipping the bacon strips once, after about 10 minutes.

3. Remove the baking sheet from the oven and lay the bacon strips on a paper towel–lined plate. Use the bacon in your favorite recipes or serve with Perfect Scrambled Eggs (page 36) and Toast (page 26) for the breakfast trifecta!

 Oven

YIELD: 8 SLICES

PREP TIME: 2 minutes
COOKING TIME: 20 minutes

1 (12–16 ounce) package of bacon

Breakfast Frittata

There's nothing wrong with a healthy dose of veggies for breakfast, and this easy-to-make frittata pulls it all together in a warm and comforting morning meal that's perfect when you need a full meal to get you going.

1. Preheat the oven to 375°F.

2. Over medium-high heat, melt the butter in a large ovenproof skillet or pot (a Dutch oven or cast-iron skillet also works well for this). When the butter has melted, add the onion and mushrooms and cook, stirring occasionally, for 5 minutes, or until the onion is slightly soft.

3. Add the ham, peppers, and spinach. Stir until well combined, then cover for 3 minutes, or until spinach is wilted. Remove from the heat.

4. In a large bowl, lightly beat the eggs, then add the shredded cheese and sour cream. Mix well.

5. Add the egg mixture to the pot and combine well. Place the pot in the preheated oven, uncovered, for 30 minutes, or until the eggs are just set and the top is lightly golden. Remove the pot from the oven and let the frittata sit for 5 minutes before serving.

 Oven

YIELD: 8 SERVINGS

PREP TIME: 15 minutes

COOKING TIME: 30 minutes

1 tablespoon butter

1 medium onion, any kind, diced

8 ounces sliced white or cremini mushrooms

½ pound sliced ham, diced

½ 12-ounce jar roasted red peppers, diced

2 cups tightly packed raw baby spinach

12 eggs

1 cup shredded Monterey Jack cheese

½ cup sour cream

Sheet Pan Chicken and Waffles

I was a little hesitant to include this recipe because it's a bit trendy and a little odd. But it's JUST. SO. GOOD. This breakfast dish is a real crowd pleaser. I hope you enjoy it as much as my family does.

1. Preheat the oven to 450°F and line a rimmed baking sheet with foil. Spray the foil with nonstick cooking spray.

2. In a large bowl, mix together the sour cream, garlic powder, 1 teaspoon of the dried thyme, the onion powder, and the cayenne pepper. Coat the chicken pieces with the mixture.

3. In another large bowl, mix together breadcrumbs, salt, pepper, and the remaining thyme and press the chicken pieces into the mixture to evenly coat them.

4. Place the chicken pieces, spaced evenly, on the baking sheet and spray the tops with additional nonstick cooking spray.

5. Bake the chicken for 15 minutes, until the pieces are lightly browned on top.

 Oven

YIELD: 6 SERVINGS

PREP TIME: 15 minutes

COOKING TIME: 30 to 35 minutes

Nonstick cooking spray

½ cup sour cream

1 teaspoon garlic powder

2 teaspoons dried thyme, divided

½ teaspoon onion powder

½ teaspoon cayenne pepper

2 to 3 pounds chicken tenders (or 4 boneless, skinless chicken breasts, sliced on an angle to make 8 thinner pieces)

ingredients continue on following page

6. Remove the baking sheet from the oven. Turn over the chicken pieces and push them to one side of the baking sheet. On the other half of the sheet, place the frozen waffles, overlapping them if necessary.

7. Bake for an additional 15 to 20 minutes, flipping the waffles as needed to ensure even baking. If more browning is desired, set the oven to broil for the last 5 minutes.

8. Serve with warm syrup.

2 cups panko breadcrumbs

1 teaspoon salt

½ teaspoon pepper

12 frozen waffles

Maple syrup for serving

Tater Tot Breakfast Casserole

There's something for everyone in this easy-to-make breakfast dish. And there's nothing like a good Tater Tot to get your day going.

1. Preheat the oven to 350°F and spray a 9 x 13-inch baking pan with nonstick cooking spray (be sure the pan fits in your RV oven).

2. Slice bacon crosswise into ½-inch pieces. In a large skillet, sauté the bacon over medium-high heat for approximately 10 minutes, or until it's fully cooked and crisp. Using a slotted spoon, transfer the bacon to a paper towel–lined plate.

3. Pour off all but 1 tablespoon of the bacon grease from the skillet. Add the onion to the skillet and cook over high heat for 2 to 3 minutes. Add the sausage to the skillet and cook for 6 to 8 minutes, or until it's crumbly and no longer pink. Add the bacon back to the skillet and mix well. Pour the sausage mixture into the prepared baking pan.

 Oven

YIELD: 8 SERVINGS

PREP TIME: 15 minutes
COOKING TIME: 45 minutes

Nonstick cooking spray

8 slices of bacon

½ medium onion, any kind, minced

1 pound ground sausage, sweet or hot

8 eggs

2 cups shredded cheddar cheese

¼ cup milk

1 (4-ounce) can diced green chiles

½ teaspoon salt

¼ teaspoon pepper

1 (16-ounce) bag frozen Tater Tots

3 green onions, chopped

4. In a large bowl, beat the eggs, and then add the cheese, milk, chiles, salt, and pepper. Mix well and pour over the sausage mixture.

5. Top the mixture with the frozen Tater Tots in a single layer.

6. Bake for 45 minutes. Let the casserole cool for 5 minutes, then garnish with green onions before serving.

Vanilla Cream Steel Cut Oatmeal with Berries

Gone are the days of standing over a hot stove stirring and stirring (and stirring) steel cut oats to perfection. The pressure cooker makes this a quick and easy "dump and go" breakfast.

1. Put the butter, oats, cream, sugar, vanilla extract, salt, and water into the pressure cooker inner pot and mix well.

2. Secure the lid, ensuring the pressure valve is turned toward the sealing position.

3. Pressure cook on high and set the time to 12 minutes.

4. When cook time is complete, let the pressure cooker naturally release (sit undisturbed) for 10 minutes. Then turn the pressure valve toward the venting position to quick-release the remaining pressure. Carefully remove the lid.

5. Stir the oatmeal well. It will thicken as it is stirred.

6. Serve immediately with your choice of toppings.

 **Instant Pot**

YIELD: 4 SERVINGS

PREP TIME: 2 minutes
COOKING TIME: 12 minutes
TOTAL TIME: 25 minutes

1 tablespoon butter

1 cup steel cut oats (not rolled or quick cooking oats)

1 cup heavy cream (or vanilla-flavored creamer)

¼ cup sugar

1 teaspoon vanilla extract (omit if using vanilla-flavored creamer)

½ teaspoon salt

2 cups water

Topping: Fresh blueberries, raspberries, almonds, or chopped walnuts (optional)

Basic Hard-Boiled Eggs

While these eggs are not exactly "boiled," they're the quickest and most consistent way to get perfect hard-boiled results every time. Plus, they peel like a dream.

1. Place the steam rack into the pressure cooker inner pot and add ¾ cup of water.

2. Place the eggs on top of the rack in a single layer.

3. Secure the lid and turn the pressure valve toward the sealing position.

4. Pressure cook on high pressure for 7 minutes.

5. When cook time is complete, turn the pressure valve toward the venting position to quick-release the pressure. Carefully remove the lid.

6. Remove the eggs with tongs and place them in a medium bowl with cool water until they can be handled easily.

7. Peel the eggs and serve them with salt and pepper. The eggs will peel easiest soon after cooking.

 Instant Pot

YIELD: 6 EGGS

PREP TIME: 2 minutes
COOKING TIME: 7 minutes
TOTAL TIME: 15 minutes

6 eggs
Salt and pepper to taste

LUNCH & SNACKS

No-Bake Protein Balls

These protein balls are full of wholesome goodness and make a great snack to take on a daylong excursion—hiking, fishing, or even on a long walk to enjoy the scenery.

1. Place the oats, honey, chocolate chips, peanut butter, and vanilla in a medium bowl and mix well. Cover and refrigerate for 30 minutes.

2. Remove the bowl from the refrigerator. Coat your hands with butter or oil to prevent sticking while rolling the mixture into balls. Spoon approximately 1½ tablespoons of the mixture into the palm of your hand and roll it into a compact ball. Repeat until all the mixture has been used.

3. Let cool for at least 30 minutes. Store the protein balls in the refrigerator for up to a week or freeze for up to 3 months for later use.

YIELD: 12 BALLS

PREP TIME: 15 minutes
COOKING TIME: 0 minutes

1 cup rolled oats

¼ cup honey

¼ cup candy-coated mini chocolate chips

⅓ cup peanut butter or almond butter

½ teaspoon vanilla extract

Charcuterie Board

Yes, it sounds fancy—but a platter of charcuterie is one of our favorite things to enjoy for lunch on a beautiful day. I load it up with a generous assortment of meats, cheeses, nuts, and dried fruit, and everyone gets to pick and choose what they love best. Then I use the leftovers (if there are any) for sandwiches the next day.

1. On a large platter or cutting board, arrange rolled or folded meat in the center of the board.
2. Around the meats, pile the cheese cubes. Add the soft cheese, placing a spreading knife next to it.
3. Place small piles of nuts between the meats and cheeses.
4. Sprinkle the cheese with the dried fruit if you like.
5. Serve with your choice of bread or crackers.

YIELD: 4 SERVINGS

PREP TIME: 15 minutes
COOKING TIME: 0 minutes

½ pound prosciutto, sliced thin

½ pound sliced hard salami

½ pound sliced Genoa salami (or sliced turkey)

4 ounces Swiss cheese, sliced or cubed

4 ounces cheddar cheese, cubed

4 ounces soft cheese (goat, Brie, Camembert)

1 cup nuts of choice (we like candied walnuts, pistachios, and smoked almonds)

ingredients continue on following page

½ cup dried cranberries, or other dried fruit

Baguettes (or any bread you like), crackers, Melba toast, or large croutons for serving

Dried fruit, optional

Ham Rolls

This one takes me back to my childhood. My mom used to make these ham rolls for us when she needed to pull together a quick and easy no-cook snack or lunch. We always loved it! I make it exactly like she did. Thanks, Mom.

1. In a medium bowl, mix together the cream cheese, Worcestershire sauce, green onions, and a bit of salt and pepper until well blended.

2. Spread 1 tablespoon of the cream cheese spread on each slice of ham. Roll the ham tightly and stack the rolls on a plate, seam side down. Enjoy with Summer Veggie Packets (page 153)!

YIELD: 6 SNACK SERVINGS

PREP TIME: 10 minutes

COOKING TIME: 0 minutes

12 ounces whipped cream cheese, softened

1 teaspoon Worcestershire sauce

2 green onions, chopped

Salt and pepper to taste

1 pound thick-sliced deli ham (about 12 to 20 slices)

BLT Sandwiches

Crisp bacon is the key to high-quality BLTs. The recipe for Oven-Baked Bacon (on page 43) will make all the difference. Crispy and cool lettuce is another essential ingredient, and don't forget the salt and pepper. Avocado slices are a nice addition to this classic camping lunch.

1. In a small bowl, mix mayonnaise and seasoned salt. Spread the mixture over one side of each of 4 pieces of toast.

2. On the mayonnaise side of the toast, place 4 tomato slices so that they overlap one another. Add a leaf of lettuce and 3 slices of bacon.

3. Season with salt and pepper, if you like. Top with the remaining 4 slices of toast. Cut the sandwiches in half and serve.

YIELD: 4 SANDWICHES

PREP TIME: 10 minutes

COOKING TIME: 0 minutes (except bacon)

3 tablespoons mayonnaise

½ teaspoon seasoned salt

8 slices of Toast (page 26)

4 small Roma tomatoes, sliced

4 leaves crunchy lettuce

12 slices Oven-Baked Bacon (page 43)

Salt and pepper to taste

Shredded Chicken Tacos

A taco bar is always a huge hit when we're on the road, but don't let that stop you from using this flavorful shredded chicken on nachos or a stuffed baked potato.

1. Place the chicken in the pressure cooker inner pot and add the chicken broth. Sprinkle taco seasoning over the chicken. Secure the lid, ensuring the pressure valve is turned toward the sealing position, and pressure cook on high pressure for 7 minutes.

2. When cook time is complete, turn the pressure valve toward the venting position to quick-release the pressure. Carefully remove the lid. Using two forks, shred the chicken right in the pot. Place the chicken in a gallon-size resealable plastic bag and add about a cup of the liquid. Securely seal the bag.

3. Store the bag of chicken in the refrigerator for up to 5 days or in the freezer for up to 3 months.

 Make Ahead

YIELD: 8 TACOS

PREP TIME: 15 minutes
COOKING TIME: 7 minutes
TOTAL TIME: 30 minutes

1½ pounds boneless, skinless chicken breasts or thighs, cut into 4-inch pieces

1 cup chicken broth (or water)

1 packet taco seasoning

8 taco shells (hard or soft)

Toppings: Diced tomatoes, radishes, cucumber, red onion, shredded lettuce, cilantro, lime juice, sour cream or chiptole sauce (all optional)

4. To serve the tacos, warm the chicken in a pot on the cooktop until heated through, approximately 10 minutes.

5. Serve the chicken in taco shells with the toppings of your choice.

Sloppy Joes

The list of ingredients in this dish may look daunting, but the tangy, hearty, slightly sweet end result makes it well worth it. And the ingredients are all pantry staples that you'll most likely have on hand.

1. Heat the oil for about a minute in a large pot over medium-high heat. Add the onion and celery and sauté about 5 minutes, or until vegetables are soft.

2. Add the ground beef to the pot and brown the meat for 6 to 8 minutes, or until it's cooked through.

3. Add all the remaining ingredients. Bring the mixture to a boil, then let it simmer for 5 minutes. Serve on toasted buns.

 Cooktop

YIELD: 4 SANDWICHES

PREP TIME: 10 minutes
COOKING TIME: 10 minutes

1 tablespoon vegetable oil

½ medium onion, any kind, chopped

2 stalks celery, finely chopped

1 pound lean ground beef

2 cloves garlic, minced

1 (15-ounce) can crushed tomatoes

½ cup ketchup

2 tablespoons tomato paste

1 tablespoon Worcestershire sauce

1 tablespoon brown sugar

ingredients continue on following page

1 tablespoon white
wine vinegar

1 teaspoon dried
oregano

1 teaspoon salt

½ teaspoon pepper

Several dashes hot
pepper sauce to taste
(optional)

4 oversized hamburger
buns, toasted

Stovetop Chili

This chili is go-to comfort food on a cool camping night when you don't want to spend hours cooking—and it's easy to make with pantry staples you'll likely always have on hand.

1. Place the butter in a large pot over high heat. Add the onion and jalapeño. Cook the mixture, stirring occasionally, for 5 minutes, or until the onion begins to soften. Add the ground beef and cook for 5 to 10 minutes, or until the meat is crumbly and no longer pink.

2. Add the tomatoes, kidney beans, chili powder, garlic powder, and salt to the pot. Stir and bring the mixture to a boil; then reduce the heat and simmer, covered, for 15 minutes. Serve the chili in bowls and use the topping(s) you like best.

 Cooktop

YIELD: 6 SERVINGS

PREP TIME: 10 minutes

COOKING TIME: 30 minutes

1 tablespoon butter (or olive oil)

1 medium onion, any kind, diced

1 jalapeño pepper, seeded and minced

1 pound lean ground beef

2 (15-ounce) cans diced tomatoes with juices

2 (15-ounce) cans red kidney beans, drained and rinsed

2 tablespoons chili powder

1 teaspoon garlic powder

1 teaspoon salt

Toppings: Shredded cheddar cheese, sour cream, sliced jalapeño pepper (optional)

Turkey Lettuce Wraps

When you're in the mood for a light but nourishing lunch, these easy-to-make turkey lettuce wraps hit the spot. Crisp iceberg lettuce is my favorite for the wraps, but Bibb or romaine work just as well.

1. Place a large skillet over medium-high heat. Add the olive oil and sesame oil, and then add the ground turkey. Sauté 6 to 7 minutes, breaking the meat into small pieces as it cooks.

2. Add the red pepper flakes, if using, white and light green parts of the green onions, garlic, ginger, and water chestnuts. Stir together and sauté for 2 minutes. Add the hoisin sauce, soy sauce, rice wine vinegar, and chicken broth. Stir to combine. Bring the mixture to a simmer and cook another 2 to 3 minutes.

3. Using a slotted spoon, transfer the turkey mixture to a serving platter and top with the remaining chopped green onions. Spoon the turkey mixture into the middle of each lettuce leaf and serve.

 Cooktop

YIELD: 4 SERVINGS

PREP TIME: 15 minutes
COOKING TIME: 10 minutes

1 tablespoon olive oil

1 teaspoon sesame oil

1 pound ground turkey

½ teaspoon red pepper flakes (optional)

3 green onions, chopped

2 cloves garlic, minced

1 tablespoon chopped ginger

1 (8-ounce) can sliced water chestnuts, drained and chopped

4 tablespoons hoisin sauce

2 tablespoons soy sauce

1 teaspoon rice wine vinegar

½ cup chicken broth

8 leaves iceberg lettuce

Baked Brats with Onions and Peppers

For years, I grilled brats. But then one time when I ran out of propane for the grill, I put them in the oven. Lightbulb moment! Best brats ever! They cook perfectly every time and cleanup is a breeze.

1. Preheat the oven to 400°F. Line a rimmed baking sheet with foil.

2. In a large bowl, toss the bell peppers and onion with the oil, salt, and pepper, and then spread them out on the baking sheet in a single layer.

3. Nestle the bratwurst into the peppers and onions.

4. Bake the mixture in the oven for 15 minutes, and then flip the bratwursts and stir the peppers and onions.

5. Cook an additional 10 minutes, until the peppers and onions are soft, and the brats are cooked through.

6. Serve with brown mustard in a hoagie roll if using.

 Oven

YIELD: 4 SANDWICHES

PREP TIME: 10 minutes

COOKING TIME: 25 minutes

1 red bell pepper, cored, seeded, and cut into ¼-inch strips

1 green bell pepper, cored, seeded, and cut into ¼-inch strips

1 medium onion, any kind, peeled and sliced into ¼-inch strips

2 tablespoons extra-virgin olive oil

1 teaspoon salt

½ teaspoon pepper

4 bratwurst sausages

4 large hoagie rolls (optional)

Topping: Brown mustard (optional)

Crispy Oven-Baked Wings

I've never met a chicken wing I didn't like, so I wanted to make sure my family could enjoy an easy version every time we go RVing. The key to crispy wings is to pat them very dry before seasoning them. Serve the wings with ranch or blue cheese dressing or feel free to toss them in your favorite buffalo sauce.

1. Preheat the oven to 450°F.

2. Pat the wings with a paper towel until they're very dry.

3. In a small bowl, mix the baking powder, salt, black pepper, and cayenne pepper. Toss the wings with the seasonings (in a bowl or a gallon-size resealable plastic bag) until they're well coated.

4. Line a rimmed baking sheet with foil or spray the sheet with nonstick cooking spray for easy cleanup. Fit a wire rack inside the baking sheet.

5. Place the coated wings on the rack and bake for 30 minutes, turning the wings halfway through the cooking time to ensure even cooking.

 Oven

YIELD: 10 WINGS

PREP TIME: 5 minutes

COOKING TIME: 30 minutes

1 pound chicken wings, thawed

1 tablespoon baking powder

1 teaspoon salt

½ teaspoon black pepper

¼ teaspoon cayenne pepper (optional)

Ranch or blue cheese dressing or buffalo sauce (optional)

Nonstick cooking spray

6. If extra crispiness is desired, place the wings skin side up under the broiler for 5 minutes.

7. Serve the wings with ranch or blue cheese dressing or buffalo sauce.

Hawaiian Chicken Skewers

Chicken and pineapple are a match made in heaven. And the drizzle of BBQ sauce takes these Hawaiian chicken skewers to a whole new level.

1. In a medium bowl, whisk together the ingredients for the sauce. Reserve half of the sauce to a small bowl to use later for basting. Place the chicken pieces in the medium bowl with the sauce, coat well, then refrigerate the bowl for 30 minutes.

2. Soak 8 wooden skewers for 30 minutes or use metal skewers.

3. Preheat the grill to medium-high and close the lid while it heats up.

4. Thread the chicken, pineapple, bell peppers, and onion onto the skewers, alternating ingredients.

5. Place the skewers on the grill and close the lid. Cook 10 minutes. Baste with the reserved sauce. Turn over the skewers and close the lid again to cook for 10 minutes. Open the lid and baste again. Remove the skewers and serve.

 Grill

YIELD: 4 SERVINGS

PREP TIME: 20 minutes
COOKING TIME: 20 minutes

FOR THE SAUCE

1 cup **BBQ** sauce

½ cup soy sauce

¼ cup reserved pineapple juice

Pinch cayenne pepper (optional)

FOR THE CHICKEN

1½ pounds boneless, skinless chicken breasts, cut into 1½-inch pieces

1 (20-ounce) can pineapple chunks in 100 percent juice, juice reserved

2 bell peppers (any color), cored, seeded, and cut into 1½-inch squares

1 onion, any kind, cut into wedges

Frozen Hamburgers Done Right

Don't laugh. Frozen burgers have their place in RV travel. These make for a quick and easy midday meal that everyone loves. The key is not to overcook the burgers and to serve them with fresh, crisp toppings.

1. Preheat the grill to medium-high and close the lid while it heats up.

2. Season both sides of the frozen hamburger patties with seasoned salt.

3. Drizzle the onion rings with the oil and sprinkle with salt and pepper.

4. When the grill has reached temperature, place the hamburger patties on one side of the grill and the onion rings on the other. Close the lid.

5. Cook for approximately 5 minutes, until juices just begin to form on top of the patties. Flip the patties and cook an additional 4 minutes. Turn the onions over when you turn the burgers over, or as the onions begin to char. Close the lid.

6. Add a slice of cheese to each hamburger, if using, and close the lid for another 2 minutes.

 Grill

YIELD: 4 HAMBURGERS

PREP TIME: 15 minutes
COOKING TIME: 10 minutes

4 frozen hamburger patties, ¼ pound each

1 tablespoon seasoned salt

½ medium onion, any kind, sliced into rings

1 tablespoon oil

½ teaspoon salt

½ teaspoon pepper

4 slices American cheese (optional)

4 hamburger buns

Toppings: Lettuce, tomato, ketchup, mustard, mayo

7. Transfer the burgers to a platter but leave the onions on the grill. Place the hamburger buns, facedown, on the grill. Close the lid and cook 1 to 2 minutes, until the buns are lightly toasted.

8. Remove the buns and onions. Build the cheeseburgers with the desired toppings and serve.

Grilled Chicken Tender Sandwiches

This sandwich was born out of necessity, when I was in a "what's left in the fridge that I need to cook" moment. And the result quickly became one of our all-time favorites. The mild flavors blend perfectly, and two tenders are just the right size for each sandwich.

1. Preheat the grill to medium-high heat and close the lid while it heats up.

2. Salt and pepper the chicken tenders, then lay them on the grill in pairs, touching side by side. (You'll have four sets of two tenders, a pair for each of the sandwiches.) Close the grill and cook the chicken tenders for 5 minutes.

3. Flip the chicken tenders and top each pair with a slice of Swiss cheese. Place ciabatta rolls facedown on the grill to toast. Close the lid for another 3 or 4 minutes. Check to make sure the chicken is fully cooked, no longer pink in the middle with juices running clear. Remove the ciabatta rolls.

4. Spread mayonnaise on the grilled side of the top roll. Place the grilled tenders on the grilled side of the bottom roll. Add sliced avocado on the chicken, cover with the top roll, and serve.

 Grill

YIELD: 4 SANDWICHES

PREP TIME: 5 minutes

COOKING TIME: 10 minutes

8 chicken tenders (about 1 pound)

Salt and pepper to taste

4 slices Swiss cheese

4 tablespoons mayonnaise

4 ciabatta rolls, sliced

1 ripe avocado, pitted and sliced

Chili Cheese Dogs

This easy-peasy recipe is a longtime classic. Just make sure to have lots of napkins around when it's time to eat!

1. Preheat the grill to high and close the lid while it heats up.

2. When the grill has reached temperature, place the hot dogs on the grill and cook with the lid closed for 6 to 8 minutes, turning every 2 minutes.

3. During the last 2 minutes of cooking, move the hot dogs to one side of the grill. Place hot dog buns facedown on the grill to toast.

4. Remove the hot dogs and buns. To serve, place a hot dog in a bun and top with warm chili. Sprinkle with cheese and onion and add relish and mustard, if using.

 Grill

YIELD: 4 SANDWICHES

PREP TIME: 5 minutes

COOKING TIME: 6–8 minutes

4 hot dogs

4 hot dog buns

2 cups Stovetop Chili (page 00) or canned chili

1 cup shredded cheddar cheese (optional)

½ medium onion, any kind, peeled and diced (optional)

Toppings: Relish and mustard (optional)

Grilled BBQ Chicken Drumsticks and Thighs

Chicken drumsticks and thighs have tons of flavor because they have more fat than breasts do. It is important to keep an eye on them as they cook, however, so that the fat drippings don't cause flare-ups in your grill. A quick spritz with a water bottle comes in handy, should you get a flare—and you'll be devouring your grilled chicken in no time.

1. Preheat the grill to medium heat and close the lid while it heats up.

2. Pat the chicken pieces dry and sprinkle them all over with the seasoned salt, salt, and pepper.

3. In a small bowl, add ½ cup water to the BBQ sauce to thin it out. Set it aside.

4. When the grill has reached temperature, place the chicken pieces on the grill and close the lid for 20 minutes, turning the pieces once during this time.

5. Open the lid and brush the chicken pieces with the sauce. Close the lid and cook another 20 minutes, turning the pieces and brushing on more BBQ sauce once during this time.

 Grill

YIELD: 4 SERVINGS

PREP TIME: 5 minutes

COOKING TIME: 40 minutes

8 chicken drumsticks and thighs (4 of each), bone in, skin on

1 tablespoon seasoned salt

1 teaspoon salt

1 teaspoon pepper

1 cup BBQ sauce, store-bought or homemade

6. After a total of 40 minutes, turn the heat up to high and brush the chicken with more sauce, turning the pieces for even cooking. Remove the chicken when it is lightly charred, the meat is no longer pink, and the juices run clear.

7. Let the chicken sit for 5 minutes before serving.

Beef and Tomato Skewers

Beef and tomatoes go together like mac and cheese—a perfect marriage. Make sure to spear the tomatoes directly in the center, so they stay on the skewer as you turn them over on the grill.

1. Soak 8 wooden skewers for 30 minutes or use metal skewers.

2. Preheat the grill to medium-high and close the lid while it heats up.

3. Thread the beef, tomatoes, and onion onto the skewers, evenly distributing them.

4. Drizzle the loaded skewers with oil, and then sprinkle the seasonings on all sides.

5. Place the skewers on the grill and cook 10 to 12 minutes, turning the skewers regularly to ensure even cooking.

6. Remove the skewers from the grill and let them sit for 5 minutes before serving.

 Grill

YIELD: 4 SERVINGS

PREP TIME: 15 minutes
COOKING TIME: 12 minutes

2 pounds top sirloin steak, cut into 1½-inch pieces

1 pint cherry tomatoes, rinsed

1 medium onion, any kind, cut into wedges

1 tablespoon extra-virgin olive oil

2 tablespoons steak seasoning or sauce of choice (or salt and pepper)

Quick Philly Cheesesteak Sandwiches

For these tasty sandwiches, the pressure cooker makes quick work of cooking wonderfully soft peppers and onions without overcooking the beef. Don't skip the toasting part!

1. Select the sauté function to heat the pressure cooker inner pot. Add the oil to coat the bottom of the pot. Add the bell pepper, onion, salt, and black pepper. Sauté for approximately 4 minutes, or until the onion starts to soften.

2. Turn off the Sauté function and add the steak strips. Add ½ cup of water. Stir to combine. Secure the lid, ensuring the pressure valve is turned toward the sealing position. Pressure cook on high pressure for 4 minutes.

3. When the cook time is complete, turn the pressure valve toward the venting position to quick-release the pressure. Carefully remove the lid and stir the ingredients.

4. Turn on the oven broiler. Open the hoagie rolls and place them faceup on a baking sheet. Using tongs,

 Instant Pot

YIELD: 4 SANDWICHES

PREP TIME: 15 minutes

COOKING TIME: 10 minutes

TOTAL TIME: 40 minutes
(including pressure and broiler time)

1 tablespoon extra-virgin olive oil

1 medium bell pepper, cored, seeded, and cut into ½-inch slices

1 medium onion, any kind, cut into ½-inch slices

1 teaspoon salt

½ teaspoon black pepper

2 pounds strip steak, thinly sliced against the grain

4 hoagie rolls

4 slices Provolone cheese

evenly divide the beef mixture and place a portion on top of one side of each hoagie roll. Top each sandwich with a slice of cheese, covering the beef completely.

5. Place the baking sheet under the broiler for 3 to 5 minutes to toast the sandwiches. Remove them from the broiler as soon as the cheese melts. Close the sandwiches and serve immediately.

Loaded Potato Soup

Pull this one out on a cool spring or fall evening when you need a bowl full of awesomeness. It's a rich and satisfying meal that goes well with sitting around a campfire.

1. Turn on the pressure cooker to sauté mode and wait until the pot is hot. Add the butter and onion to the pot. Sauté for approximately 4 minutes, or until the onion is just turning soft.

2. Add garlic and sauté another minute.

3. Add the potatoes, broth, frozen broccoli, salt, pepper, and cayenne pepper, if using. Mix well. Turn off the sauté function and secure the lid, ensuring the pressure valve is turned toward sealing. Pressure cook on high pressure for 6 minutes.

4. When cook time is complete, let the pressure cooker naturally release (sit undisturbed) for 3 minutes. Then turn the pressure valve toward the venting position to quick-release the remaining pressure.

5. Carefully remove the lid and turn on the sauté function. At this point, you can either leave the mixture chunky

 Instant Pot

YIELD: 4 SERVINGS

PREP TIME: 10 minutes
COOKING TIME: 11 minutes
TOTAL TIME: 30 minutes

2 tablespoons butter

1 medium onion, any kind, diced

2 cloves garlic, minced

3 pounds Yukon Gold potatoes, unpeeled and diced

4 cups chicken broth (or vegetable broth)

1 (16-ounce) package frozen broccoli

2 teaspoons kosher salt

½ teaspoon black pepper

¼ teaspoon cayenne pepper (optional)

ingredients continue on following page

or use an immersion blender for 1–2 minutes to make the texture smooth. I prefer to leave it chunky.

6. Add the slurry to the pot and stir well until the soup just starts to thicken.

7. Add the sour cream and shredded cheese and mix well. Turn off the heat. Serve the soup in bowls and top with crumbled bacon, chives, and more shredded cheese and sour cream, if you like.

2 tablespoons cornstarch mixed with 2 tablespoons water to make a slurry

1 cup sour cream

1 cup shredded sharp cheddar cheese

Toppings: Crumbled bacon, chives, additional shredded cheddar cheese, additional sour cream

Shredded Chicken Gyros

These easy chicken gyros are a refreshing change of pace when it comes to camping food, and the cucumbers and dill will brighten up everyone's day.

FOR THE SAUCE

1. Using a box grater, shred half of the cucumber into a paper towel–lined medium bowl. Sprinkle the cucumber with salt, let sit for 15 minutes, then press out any remaining water. The cucumber should be as dry as possible. Remove the paper towel.

2. Add the yogurt, half of the lemon juice, 2 cloves of minced garlic, remaining 1 teaspoon of salt, the dill, and the olive oil to the bowl with the cucumber. Blend well and refrigerate until ready to serve.

FOR THE CHICKEN GYROS

1. Place the chicken, remaining half of the lemon juice, remaining 3 cloves of the minced garlic, remaining 2 teaspoons of the salt, the black pepper, allspice, oregano, and cayenne pepper, plus ½ cup of

 **Instant Pot**

YIELD: 8 SERVINGS

PREP TIME: 20 minutes

COOKING TIME: 20 minutes

TOTAL TIME: 45 minutes
(including pressure time)

FOR THE SAUCE

1 large or 2 small cucumbers (English cucumbers are best), half shredded and half sliced into thin coins

2 cups plain Greek yogurt

Juice of 2 lemons, divided

5 cloves garlic, minced, divided

3 teaspoons salt, divided

1 tablespoon fresh dill, chopped (or 1 teaspoon dried dill)

2 teaspoons extra-virgin olive oil

ingredients continue on following page

water in the inner pot of a pressure cooker. Secure the lid, turn the pressure valve toward the sealing position, and pressure cook on high pressure for 7 minutes.

2. When cook time is complete, let the pressure cooker naturally release (sit undisturbed) for 10 minutes. Turn the pressure valve toward the venting position to quick-release the remaining pressure. Carefully remove the lid and shred the chicken with two forks. Leave the chicken in the juices, with the pressure cooker lid on, until you're ready to serve.

3. Preheat the oven to 250°F with a rack set in the middle position. Or preheat a grill to low heat with the lid closed while it warms up.

4. When the oven comes to temperature, place the pita breads on the middle rack for 10 minutes, or until warm.

5. Remove the pressure cooker lid. Using tongs, remove the chicken, transferring it to a serving platter. Serve with the sauce and toppings.

FOR THE CHICKEN GYROS

2 pounds boneless, skinless chicken breasts, cut crosswise into ½-inch-wide fingers

1 teaspoon black pepper

1 teaspoon allspice

1 teaspoon dried oregano

½ teaspoon cayenne pepper

8 whole pitas

Toppings: Remaining thinly sliced cucumber, thinly sliced tomato, thinly sliced red onion, chopped romaine lettuce

Carolina-Style BBQ Chicken Sandwiches

Here's another light lunch that comes together in a pinch. The tang of the vinegar and the sweetness of the sugar are beautifully balanced and leave you with a mouthful of flavor. These sandwiches are balanced perfectly with Easy Coleslaw (page 143).

1. Place the chicken, broth, vinegar, sugar, and red pepper flakes in the pressure cooker inner pot and stir. Secure the lid, ensuring that the pressure valve is set to the sealing position, then pressure cook on high pressure for 7 minutes. When the cook time is complete, turn the pressure valve toward the venting position to quick-release the pressure.

2. Carefully remove the lid, then remove the chicken to a medium bowl. Keep 1 cup of the liquid in the pot and pour the rest into a small bowl and set aside.

3. Turn on the pot to sauté mode and heat liquid for approximately 15 minutes, or until it reduces by half. Turn off the pressure cooker.

 **Instant Pot**

YIELD: 4 SANDWICHES

PREP TIME: 15 minutes
COOKING TIME: 7 minutes
TOTAL TIME: 30 minutes
(including pressure time)

1½ pounds boneless, skinless chicken breasts, cut into 4- to 5-inch pieces

¾ cup chicken broth

¼ cup white wine vinegar

¼ cup sugar

1 teaspoon red pepper flakes

1 teaspoon salt

4 brioche buns

4. Shred the chicken with two forks and place it back in the pot with the reduced sauce and stir. Keep the chicken warm with the pressure cooker lid on.

5. Turn on the oven broiler. Add the salt and stir. Open the buns and toast them under the broiler for 3 to 4 minutes.

6. Pile chicken onto one side of each toasted bun and serve warm. Drizzle some of the liquid from the pot over the chicken.

Pulled Pork Pizza

I can't count how many times I've made this pizza. It's just that good!

1. Place the pork, onion, ½ cup of the BBQ sauce, bay leaf, salt, pepper, garlic, and reserved pineapple juice into the inner pot of the pressure cooker. Stir to combine.

2. Secure the lid, ensuring the pressure valve is turned toward the sealing position. Pressure cook on high pressure for 60 minutes. When cook time is complete, let the pressure cooker naturally release (sit undisturbed) for 15 minutes. Then turn the pressure valve toward the venting position to quick-release the remaining pressure.

3. Preheat the oven to 450°F.

4. Carefully remove the lid from the pressure cooker. Remove the pork from the pot. Using two forks, shred it in a large bowl. Remove any large pieces of fat.

5. In the same bowl with the shredded pork, add the remaining ½ cup of BBQ sauce and the pineapple and

 Instant Pot

YIELD: 4 SERVINGS

PREP TIME: 15 minutes

COOKING TIME: 90 minutes

TOTAL TIME: 2 hours
(including pressure time)

2- to 3-pound boneless pork butt (shoulder), trimmed and cut into large chunks

1 medium onion, any kind, cut into wedges

1 cup BBQ sauce, divided, plus more for serving

1 bay leaf

2 teaspoons salt

1 teaspoon pepper

3 cloves garlic, smashed

1 (20-ounce) can pineapple tidbits, drained and juice reserved

1 (12-inch) prebaked pizza crust such as Boboli®

combine. Spread the mixture over the entire pizza crust and bake directly on the oven rack 10 to 15 minutes, or until the crust's edges brown.

6. Remove the pizza from the oven and let it sit for 5 minutes. Drizzle any remaining BBQ sauce over the top, if desired. Cut and serve.

DINNER

Beef Enchilada Bake

This recipe highlights my Arizona heritage and is one of my favorite make-ahead camping meals. Classic Southwestern flavors, topped with cool tomatoes and sour cream, make it a true crowd-pleaser.

1. Place a large skillet over high heat and add the oil. Add the onion and sauté for 3 to 5 minutes, or until the onion is just turning soft. Add the ground beef and cook 6 to 8 minutes, or until the meat is crumbly and no longer pink.

2. Add the pinto beans and taco seasoning. Stir well. Remove from heat.

3. Spray a 9 x 13-inch disposable baking pan with nonstick cooking spray (be sure the pan fits in your RV oven).

4. Pour one-third of the enchilada sauce onto the bottom of the baking pan and layer one-third of the tortillas on the sauce.

5. Top the tortillas with half of the beef mixture and then one-third of the cheese. Top with one-third of the tortillas, one-third of the sauce, the

 Make Ahead

YIELD: 8 SERVINGS

PREP TIME: 20 minutes
COOKING TIME: 40 minutes

1 tablespoon extra-virgin olive oil

1 medium onion, any kind, diced

1 pound lean ground beef

1 (15-ounce) can pinto beans, drained and rinsed

1 packet taco seasoning

Nonstick cooking spray

1 (15-ounce) can red enchilada sauce

10 small corn tortillas cut in half, white or yellow corn

ingredients continue on following page

rest of the beef, and one-third of the cheese. Layer the last third of the tortillas, the rest of the sauce, and the rest of the cheese. Top with the olives.

6. If you're making this dish ahead of time, cover it tightly with foil and freeze for up to 3 months.

7. Move the dish from the freezer to the refrigerator the day before serving—and take it out of the fridge 1 hour before cooking.

8. Preheat the oven to 350°F and bake, covered, for 40 minutes. Remove the cover and bake another 10 to 15 minutes, until the cheese is bubbling.

9. Let the dish sit for 10 minutes, then top with the diced tomatoes. Serve with sour cream, if using.

2 cups shredded cheddar cheese

4 ounces sliced black olives, drained

2 Roma tomatoes, diced

Sour cream (optional)

Meatloaf Muffins

There's nothing like digging into homemade meatloaf while sitting by a roaring campfire, and these make-ahead meatloaf muffins make an easy dinner.

1. Preheat the oven on to 400°F. Spray a twelve-cup muffin tin with nonstick cooking spray.

2. Place a medium skillet over medium-high heat and add the olive oil. Then add the celery, carrots, and onion. Sauté for 4 to 5 minutes, or until the onion is slightly soft. Add the garlic and sauté for one more minute.

3. Place the ground beef and sausage in a large bowl and mix in the cooked vegetable mixture. Add ½ cup of the BBQ sauce, the eggs, salt, pepper, green onions, heavy cream, Worcestershire sauce, hot sauce, and breadcrumbs, if using. Mix well using your hands, but do not overmix or the meat will get tough.

4. Fill each muffin cup to just above the rim with the meat mixture.

 **Make Ahead**

YIELD: 6 SERVINGS

PREP TIME: 25 minutes
COOKING TIME: 20 minutes

Nonstick cooking spray

2 tablespoons olive oil

1 celery stalk, finely chopped

¼ cup baby carrots, finely chopped

½ medium onion, any kind, finely chopped

2 cloves garlic, minced

1 pound lean ground beef

1 pound spicy ground sausage (I prefer hot Italian)

1 cup BBQ sauce, divided

2 eggs, lightly beaten

ingredients continue on page 95

5. If you're serving the meatloaf immediately, place it in the hot oven and bake for 20 minutes. Top each muffin with a tablespoon of the reserved BBQ sauce and put the tin back in the oven for another 10 to 15 minutes.

6. If you're making the meatloaf ahead of time and freezing it, do not add the BBQ sauce after 20 minutes. Just cook the meatloaf for the entire time with no sauce on top. When the cooking time is complete, carefully remove the meatloaf muffins from the pan and let them cool on a wire rack to room temperature. Wrap the meatloaf muffins individually in foil and freeze them for up to 3 months.

7. Move the meatloaf muffins from the freezer to the refrigerator the night before serving.

8. Reheat the meatloaf in a 350°F oven for 30 minutes. For the last 10 minutes of cooking time, add some of the additional BBQ sauce to the top of each meatloaf muffin by peeling back the foil to expose the top. Serve hot.

1 teaspoon salt

½ teaspoon pepper

1 green onion, white and green parts, chopped

½ cup heavy cream

2 teaspoons Worcestershire sauce

Several dashes hot pepper sauce (optional)

1 cup breadcrumbs

Loaded Baked Potato Casserole

This casserole is the all-time most popular recipe on my blog and YouTube channel, so I just had to include it here. I make it for every RV trip, at the insistence of my entire family.

1. Preheat the oven to 375°F. Grease a 9 x 13-inch baking dish with either butter or nonstick cooking spray. (Be sure the pan fits in your RV oven.)

2. Place the unpeeled potatoes in a large pot and add enough water to cover the potatoes. Place the pot over high heat and boil approximately 15 minutes, or until the potatoes are fork tender. Drain.

3. While the potatoes are cooking, fry the bacon pieces in a large skillet over medium-high heat for 5 to 7 minutes, or until the bacon is crisp. Remove the bacon pieces with a slotted spoon and transfer them to a paper towel–lined plate. Reserve the bacon grease.

4. Place the cooked potatoes in the prepared baking dish in a single layer. There should be a little space between each potato. Using the bottom of a

 Make Ahead

YIELD: 8 SERVINGS

PREP TIME: 20 minutes

COOKING TIME: 45 minutes

Butter or nonstick cooking spray

2 pounds baby potatoes, approximately 15 to 20

1 pound bacon, sliced crosswise into ½-inch pieces

1 whole, cooked rotisserie chicken, meat removed and shredded

1 (12-ounce) bag frozen broccoli, warmed in a microwave or on the stovetop, drained

1 bunch green onions, white and green parts, sliced crosswise

ingredients continue on following page

drinking glass, lightly press each
potato, smashing it down about
halfway. The bottom of the baking
dish should be fully covered when all
of the potatoes are smashed. Drizzle
2 to 3 tablespoons of the reserved
bacon grease over the potatoes.

1 teaspoon salt

½ teaspoon pepper

½ cup chicken broth

2 cups sour cream

2 cups shredded cheddar
cheese, divided

5. In a large bowl, mix together the shredded chicken, cooked
bacon (reserving about 2 tablespoons for garnish), broccoli,
and green onions (reserving 2 tablespoons for garnish). Add the
salt and pepper and mix well. Spread the mixture evenly over
the potatoes.

6. In a small bowl, whisk together the chicken broth, sour
cream, and 1½ cups of the shredded cheese until it is well
blended. Spread this mixture on top of the chicken mixture.

7. Cover the baking dish with aluminum foil and bake for
20 minutes, or until the casserole is heated through. Remove
the foil and top with the remaining bacon, green onions, and
cheese, and then bake another 5 to 10 minutes to fully melt
and brown the cheese. Remove the baking dish from the oven
and serve.

8. If you're making this casserole ahead of time, cover it tightly
and keep it in the freezer for up to 3 months. Thaw it in the
refrigerator the night before you want to serve it. Take the
casserole out of the fridge an hour before you want to reheat
it, and then place it, uncovered, in a 350°F oven for 45 to
60 minutes.

Shepherd's Pie, Thanksgiving Style

For many, RVing over Thanksgiving is a tradition, and this shepherd's pie has all of the classic holiday flavors in a dish that can be made ahead of time. Warm it up, add a dollop of cranberry sauce, and you're good to go.

1. Place the sweet potatoes in a large pot and fill it with water until the sweet potatoes are just covered. Place the pot over high heat and bring the water to a boil. Lower the heat, and simmer for 25 minutes, or until the sweet potatoes are tender.

2. When the sweet potatoes are cooked, drain the water and place the sweet potatoes back in the pot.

3. Add 1 teaspoon of the salt, and the butter, cream, and milk and whip using a hand mixer.

4. Grease a large aluminum foil pan with nonstick cooking spray. Or if you're serving the dish immediately, grease a 9 x 13-inch baking dish with nonstick cooking spray. (Be sure the pan fits in your RV oven.)

5. Place a large skillet over medium-high heat. Add the oil and onion.

 **Make Ahead**

YIELD: 8 SERVINGS

PREP TIME: 20 minutes
COOKING TIME: 45 minutes

3 pounds sweet potatoes, approximately 3 or 4 large, peeled and cut into 3-inch chunks

2 teaspoons salt, divided

4 tablespoons butter

½ cup heavy cream

½ cup whole milk

Nonstick cooking spray

1 tablespoon olive oil

1 medium onion, any kind, diced

2 pounds ground turkey

ingredients continue on following page

Sauté the onion for 4 minutes, or until it's slightly soft. Add the ground turkey to the skillet and cook 4 to 6 minutes, breaking up any clumps into small pieces, until the meat is cooked through and no longer pink.

6. Add Italian seasoning, Worcestershire sauce, chicken broth, the remaining 1 teaspoon salt, and the pepper. Stir to combine. Add the frozen vegetables and stir to combine and warm through.

7. Pour the mixture into the prepared baking dish. Top with spoonfuls of the mashed sweet potatoes. Spread them into an even layer, and then use a fork to produce slight peaks that will brown while baking.

8. If you're making the shepherd's pie ahead of time, cover it tightly and keep it in the freezer for up to 3 months. Thaw it in the refrigerator the night before you want to serve it. Take it out of the fridge at least an hour before you want to serve it. Place it, uncovered, in a preheated

1 tablespoon Italian seasoning

2 teaspoons Worcestershire sauce

½ cup chicken broth

½ teaspoon pepper

3 cups frozen vegetables of choice, thawed

an hour before you want to serve it. Place it, uncovered, in a preheated 350°F oven for 45 to 60 minutes, or until the sweet potatoes are lightly browned. Let the pie sit for 10 minutes before serving.

9. If you're serving the shepherd's pie immediately, place the baking dish, uncovered, in a preheated 400°F oven and bake for 30 minutes. Let the pie sit for 10 minutes before serving.

Baked Mostaccioli

This heart-warming baked pasta is very easy to make, but it tastes like something you might eat at a fancy Italian restaurant. I prefer using hot sausage, but sweet also works well.

1. Spray a 9 x 13-inch disposable baking pan with nonstick cooking spray (be sure the pan fits in your RV oven).

2. Fill a large pot with water and add 2 tablespoons of salt. Cook the pasta al dente, according to package directions. Drain the pasta and set it aside.

3. Place a large skillet over high heat. Add the oil and onion. Cook for 3 to 5 minutes, until the onion just turns soft.

4. Add the sausage, 1 teaspoon of salt, and the pepper to the skillet and cook for 6 to 8 minutes, or until the sausage is crumbly and no longer pink.

5. Add the pasta sauce to the sausage mixture and reduce the heat to medium. Stir well and heat through for 5 minutes, or until the sauce is just simmering.

 Make Ahead

YIELD: 8 SERVINGS

PREP TIME: 15 minutes
COOKING TIME: 45 minutes

Nonstick cooking spray

2 tablespoons plus
1 teaspoon salt

1 pound dry mostaccioli noodles (penne or ziti work just as well)

1 tablespoon olive oil

1 medium onion, any kind, diced

1 pound ground hot or sweet Italian sausage

1 teaspoon pepper

1 (24-ounce) jar pasta sauce of choice

2 cups shredded mozzarella cheese, divided

1 cup shredded Parmesan cheese, divided

6. Add the pasta to the skillet and stir until well combined. Pour half of the pasta mixture into the prepared baking pan. Sprinkle with 1 cup of the mozzarella cheese and ½ cup of the Parmesan cheese. Pour the remaining pasta mixture on top, then sprinkle with the remaining mozzarella and Parmesan. Cover the baking pan with aluminum foil.

7. Let the pasta cool to room temperature before placing the pan in the freezer. The pan will keep, frozen, for 3 months.

8. Remove the pan from the freezer and place it in the refrigerator overnight before serving. Remove the pan from the refrigerator and leave it on the countertop for 2 hours before heating it.

9. Preheat the oven to 350°F and place the baking dish, covered, in the oven. Bake for 30 to 40 minutes, or until the sauce bubbles on the edge of the pan. Remove the foil for the last 10 minutes of cooking to brown the top.

10. Remove the pan from the oven and let it sit for 10 minutes before serving.

Southwestern Skillet Dinner

All you need is one pan and 15 minutes to get this dish on the table—and it delivers tons of flavor. Does it get any better than that?

1. Place a large skillet over high heat and add the oil. Add the onion and sauté for 4 to 5 minutes, or until it's just softening. Add the ground beef and cook for 6 to 8 minutes, or until the meat is crumbly and no longer pink.

2. Add the taco seasoning to the beef mixture and stir well.

3. Add the beans and corn and mix well. Turn the heat down to medium and cook another 3 to 4 minutes, until the mixture is heated through.

4. Sprinkle the cheese on top. Do not stir. Top the mixture with the olives and put the lid on the skillet. Let it sit over medium heat for 2 to 3 minutes, or until the cheese melts.

5. Take the skillet off the heat and sprinkle the top with cilantro. Serve topped with sour cream and with tortilla chips on the side.

 Cooktop

YIELD: 4 SERVINGS

PREP TIME: 15 minutes

COOKING TIME: 15 minutes

1 tablespoon extra-virgin olive oil

1 medium onion, any kind, diced

1 pound lean ground beef

1 packet taco seasoning

1 (15-ounce) can black beans, drained and rinsed

1 (15-ounce) can corn, drained

1 cup shredded taco blend cheese

4 ounces sliced black olives, drained

1 bunch cilantro, rinsed and chopped

Topping: Sour cream

Orzo and Chicken Medley

This is another "what's left in the pantry that I need to use" meal that has turned into one of our favorites. It also makes great leftovers (if there are any!).

1. Place a large pot (such as a Dutch oven) over high heat and add the olive oil. Add the onion and cook until the onion starts to soften.

2. Add the chicken to the pot and cook for 4 to 6 minutes, or until the meat is crumbly and no longer pink. Add the garlic and cook one more minute.

3. Add the salt, pepper, orzo, chicken broth, and lemon juice. Stir well and bring the mixture to a simmer. Reduce the heat to medium-low, cover the pot, and simmer for 15 minutes, or until the pasta is tender.

4. When the pasta is tender, stir in the cream, artichoke hearts, and tomatoes. Stir well until the mixture is warmed through. Top with grated Parmesan cheese if you like. Serve immediately.

 Cooktop

YIELD: 4 SERVINGS

PREP TIME: 15 minutes

COOKING TIME: 20 minutes

1 tablespoon extra-virgin olive oil

1 medium onion, any kind, diced

1 pound ground chicken

2 cloves garlic, minced

1 teaspoon salt

1 teaspoon pepper

8 ounces dry orzo pasta

2 cups chicken broth

Juice of 1 lemon

¼ cup heavy cream

1 (14-ounce) can quartered artichoke hearts, drained

1 (14-ounce) can fire-roasted diced tomatoes, drained

Topping: Grated Parmesan cheese (optional)

One-Pot Creamy Sausage and Rice

Instant rice has its place. And that place is definitely in the RV kitchen. Aptly named, instant rice cooks in almost no time and uses far less water and resources than regular rice. It also makes this creamy sausage and rice dish one of the quickest and easiest one-pot RV meals out there.

1. Place a large pot (such as a Dutch oven) over medium-high heat on the cooktop and add the oil.

2. When the oil is shimmering, add the ground sausage and onion. Cook for 6 to 8 minutes, or until the onion is soft and the sausage is crumbly and no longer pink.

3. Add the cream of mushroom soup and water. Stir well to combine, and then add the salt and frozen peas. Bring the mixture to a boil.

4. Add the rice, stir well, cover the pot with a lid, and immediately turn off the heat. Let the pot sit, covered, on the cooktop (with the heat off) for 5 minutes, or until all the liquid is absorbed by the rice.

5. Stir well and serve in bowls, topped with the Parmesan cheese, if using.

 Cooktop

YIELD: 4 SERVINGS

PREP TIME: 15 minutes

COOKING TIME: 15 minutes

1 tablespoon
   extra-virgin olive oil

1 pound ground hot
   Italian sausage

1 medium onion, any
   kind, diced

1 (15-ounce) can
   condensed cream of
   mushroom soup

2½ cups water

1 teaspoon salt

1 cup frozen peas

2 cups instant rice

2 tablespoons
   Parmesan cheese,
   shredded (optional)

One-Pot Spaghetti

One of my best childhood memories is my dad making spaghetti for us every Sunday night. So I had to find a way to incorporate his rich and hearty spaghetti into our RV routine without creating too much of a mess to clean up. I nailed it with my one-pot spaghetti.

1. Place a large pot (such as a Dutch oven) on the stove over medium-high heat. Add the oil to the pot and heat for 1 minute. Add the onion and cook for about 3 minutes, or until the onion is slightly translucent. Add the garlic and cook for 1 more minute. Add the ground beef and cook for 6 to 8 minutes, or until the meat is crumbly and no longer pink.

2. Add the broth, crushed tomatoes, tomato sauce, and tomato paste. Stir well and bring to a simmer. Add the basil, oregano, and red pepper flakes and bring the mixture to a simmer.

3. Add the spaghetti and gently stir. Cook the pasta al dente, according to package directions. Serve in bowls to make it easy to eat—sitting in your camp chair!

 Cooktop

YIELD: 4 SERVINGS

PREP TIME: 15 minutes
COOKING TIME: 25 minutes

2 tablespoons olive oil

1 medium onion, any kind, chopped

3 cloves garlic, minced

1 pound lean ground beef

2 cups beef broth

1 (28-ounce) can crushed tomatoes

1 (8-ounce) can tomato sauce

1 (6-ounce) can tomato paste

1 teaspoon dried basil

1 teaspoon dried oregano

Pinch red pepper flakes

8 ounces dried spaghetti, broken in half

Sheet Pan Steak Fajitas

Tender flank steak and brightly colored peppers on a sheet pan make this dish a go-to when you want a fast, flavorful, and impressive meal.

1. Preheat the oven to 400°F.

2. In a small bowl, mix the steak slices with the taco seasoning until the meat is well coated. Set it aside.

3. In a medium bowl, mix together the bell peppers, onion, oil, salt, pepper, and cumin. Spread the mixture over the surface of the prepared baking sheet.

4. Place the baking sheet in the oven and bake for 15 minutes. Remove the baking sheet and add the steak slices, distributing them evenly, in a single layer, over the top. Put the baking sheet back in the oven for 7 to 10 minutes. For the last 5 minutes of cooking time, carefully lay the foil-wrapped tortillas on top of the baking sheet.

 Oven

YIELD: 4 SERVINGS

PREP TIME: 10 minutes
COOKING TIME: 25 minutes

1 pound skirt or flank steak, thinly sliced against the grain

2 tablespoons taco seasoning

3 bell peppers (any color), cored, seeded, and sliced into thin strips

1 medium onion, any kind, thinly sliced

2 tablespoons extra-virgin olive oil

1 teaspoon salt

½ teaspoon pepper

½ teaspoon ground cumin

ingredients continue
on following page

5. Remove the baking sheet from the oven and drizzle the steak-and-peppers mixture with lime juice. Serve the warm tortillas immediately with the steak-and-pepper mixture and your choice of toppings.

Juice of 1 lime (approximately 1 tablespoon)

8 tortillas, fajita size, stacked together and wrapped in foil

Toppings: Diced tomato, shredded lettuce, and sour cream

Sheet Pan Chicken Tenders and Veggies

If you're looking for a dish that's on the healthier side, this may be the one for you. Lots of lightly seasoned veggies and tender chicken make a tasty, light evening meal.

1. Preheat the oven to 425°F. Line a rimmed baking sheet with foil for easy cleanup.

2. In a large bowl, mix together the chicken, green and yellow squash, onion, oil, rosemary, salt, and pepper until the chicken and squash are well coated.

3. Spread the chicken mixture in a single layer onto the prepared baking sheet. Place the sheet in the oven for 25 minutes.

4. Serve with rice or orzo pasta.

 Oven

YIELD: 4 SERVINGS

PREP TIME: 10 minutes

COOKING TIME: 25 minutes

1½ pounds fresh chicken tenders

1 green squash, cut into 1-inch pieces

1 yellow squash, cut into 1½-inch pieces

½ medium onion, any kind, cut into slivers

2 tablespoons extra-virgin olive oil

1 teaspoon dried rosemary

1 teaspoon salt

½ teaspoon pepper

Basic Baked Chicken Thighs

This is my husband's all-time favorite dinner. And it's one of my all-time favorite dinners to make because it's so easy. The key is to bake the chicken at a very high temperature to crisp up the skin and then dial down the temperature for the rest of the cooking time to keep the chicken from drying out. It works every time.

1. Preheat the oven to 450°F and line a rimmed baking sheet with foil for easy cleanup.

2. Trim any excess skin off of the chicken thighs.

3. Rub the olive oil all over the chicken thighs, then sprinkle with salt and pepper.

4. Place the chicken on the prepared baking sheet and place it in the oven for 25 minutes. After 25 minutes, turn the heat down to 350°F and continue to bake for 20 minutes, or until the internal temperature of the chicken reaches 165°F.

5. For extra crispiness, during the last 5 minutes of baking, raise the oven temperature to broil.

6. Remove the baking sheet from the oven and serve the chicken immediately.

 Oven

YIELD: 4 SERVINGS

PREP TIME: 5 minutes

COOKING TIME: 45 minutes

2 pounds bone-in, skin-on chicken thighs (6 to 8 pieces)

1 tablespoon olive oil

2 teaspoons coarse salt

1 teaspoon pepper

Caprese Chicken

It's shocking how easy it is to make this impressive chicken and tomato dish—it tastes like it came straight out of a chef's kitchen! So serve it up when the in-laws come over for dinner. They'll be amazed that you "eat like this" when RVing.

1. Preheat the oven to 400°F. Spray a foil-lined rimmed baking sheet with nonstick cooking spray.

2. Cut each chicken breast in half lengthwise, to make 4 cutlets, or cut them into narrower pieces if you like.

3. In a medium bowl, mix the tomatoes with 1 tablespoon of the olive oil and the Italian seasoning until the tomatoes are well coated. Spoon the mixture onto the prepared baking sheet.

4. Nestle the pieces of chicken in a single layer between the tomatoes and sprinkle with the salt and pepper.

5. Bake for 20 minutes. While the chicken is baking, whisk together ¼ cup olive oil, the balsamic vinegar, and the dried basil.

 Oven

YIELD: 4 SERVINGS

PREP TIME: 15 minutes
COOKING TIME: 25 minutes

Nonstick cooking spray

2 boneless, skinless chicken breasts (about 1½ pounds)

1 pint cherry tomatoes

1 tablespoon plus ¼ cup extra-virgin olive oil

1 teaspoon Italian seasoning

½ teaspoon salt

¼ teaspoon pepper

¼ cup balsamic vinegar

½ teaspoon dried basil

1 (8-ounce) ball fresh mozzarella, shredded

6. After 20 minutes, remove the baking sheet from the oven and sprinkle the shredded mozzarella over the chicken. Drizzle the oil and vinegar mixture over the top.

7. Put the baking sheet back in the oven for another 5 to 7 minutes, or until the cheese starts to melt.

8. Serve the chicken topped with the tomatoes.

Stuffed Baked Potatoes

This versatile meal is an all-time family favorite. You can also use ground chicken or turkey and any vegetable you have on hand.

1. Preheat the oven to 450°F. Scrub the potatoes and pierce them several times with a fork. Place the potatoes directly on the middle rack in the oven and bake them for 60 minutes, until the potatoes are easily pierced with a fork. Depending on the size of the potatoes, baking time can be anywhere from 45 to 75 minutes.

2. Put the broccoli and a few tablespoons of water in a small pan on the cooktop. Cook the broccoli florets over medium-high heat for 5 minutes, or until the broccoli is fork-tender, then set aside.

3. In a large skillet, heat the oil over high heat and add the ground beef. Cook the beef for 6 to 8 minutes, or until it is crumbly and no longer pink. Drain off any fat, if there is excess.

 Oven

YIELD: 4 SERVINGS

PREP TIME: 15 minutes
COOKING TIME: 60 minutes

4 medium russet potatoes

2 cups broccoli florets

1 tablespoon vegetable oil

1 pound lean ground beef

½ cup beef or chicken broth

¼ cup heavy cream

1 teaspoon salt

½ teaspoon pepper

½ teaspoon Worcestershire sauce

Toppings: Butter, Oven-Baked Bacon (page 43), shredded cheddar cheese, sour cream

4. Add the chicken broth, heavy cream, salt, pepper, and Worcestershire sauce to the skillet. Stir the mixture well till it's warm throughout.

5. Place each baked potato in a bowl and slice an X in the top. Fluff the flesh of the potato with a fork.

6. Put some of the ground beef and broccoli on top of each potato. Top with butter, crumbled bacon, cheddar cheese, and sour cream.

Spicy Andouille Sausage and Red Potatoes Packet

Tender red potatoes and hot andouille sausage pair beautifully in this no muss, no fuss foil packet. Serve it with Foil Packet Broccoli on the Grill (page 155) for a great meal.

1. Preheat the oven to 425°F. Tear off four 12 x 18-inch pieces of heavy-duty aluminum foil and spray one side of each sheet with nonstick cooking spray.

2. In a medium bowl, toss the potatoes and onion with the oil, salt, and pepper.

3. Place an equal amount of the mixture onto the center of each of the four foil sheets. Top each pile of potatoes with one-quarter of the sausage coins. To create a packet, bring the long sides of the foil together, then fold twice to create a seal, leaving 1 to 2 inches of room for steam to inflate the packet during cooking. For the two remaining short sides, fold twice to finish sealing.

 Oven

YIELD: 4 SERVINGS

PREP TIME: 15 minutes

COOKING TIME: 30 minutes

Nonstick cooking spray

4 small (not baby) red potatoes, scrubbed and cut into ½-inch cubes

½ medium onion, any kind, sliced into ½-inch strips

2 teaspoons extra-virgin olive oil

½ teaspoon salt

¼ teaspoon pepper

4 fully cooked andouille sausages, sliced crosswise into coins

4. Place the packets, seam side up, in the oven for 30 minutes. Remove one from the oven and carefully open a corner. Pierce a potato with a fork to ensure doneness. If the potato is not easily pierced, bake the packets for another 5 to 10 minutes.

5. When the vegetables are done to your liking, serve the foil packets immediately with Cucumber Tomato Salad (page 145).

Foil Packet Kielbasa with Potatoes and Peppers

Easy-to-find ingredients that take up very little room in your refrigerator make this kielbasa-and-potato packet a great RV dinner staple.

1. Heat the oven to 425°F. Tear off four 12 x 18-inch pieces of heavy-duty aluminum foil and set aside.

2. Mix all ingredients, except the chicken broth, in a large bowl until well coated.

3. Place an equal amount of the mixture onto the center of each of the four foil sheets. Carefully pour ⅛ cup of broth onto the food mixture. To create a packet, bring the long sides of the foil together, then fold twice to create a seal, leaving 1 to 2 inches of room for steam to inflate the packet during cooking. For the two remaining short sides, fold twice to finish sealing.

4. Place the packets on a baking sheet and put them in the oven, seam side up, for 40 minutes.

 Oven

YIELD: 4 SERVINGS

PREP TIME: 15 minutes

COOKING TIME: 40 minutes

2 tablespoons extra-virgin olive oil

1 (14-ounce) package fully cooked Polska kielbasa, sliced crosswise into ½-inch coins

2 Yukon Gold potatoes, scrubbed and cut into 1-inch cubes

1 red bell pepper, cored, seeded, and cut into ½-inch wide strips

1 green bell pepper, cored, seeded, and cut into ½-inch wide strips

ingredients continue on following page

5. Remove a packet from the oven and carefully open a corner. Test for doneness by piercing a potato with a fork. It should be soft.

6. Pour the liquid out of the packet through the open corner.

7. When the vegetables are done to your liking, serve immediately, either in the packet or on a plate.

½ medium onion, any kind, cut into ½-inch-wide half-moon slices

Juice of 1 lemon

2 teaspoons salt

½ teaspoon black pepper

½ teaspoon Italian seasoning

½ cup chicken broth

Lemon Herb Tilapia Foil Packet

Light and lemony with a hint of dill, this tilapia foil packet is just right for those hot summer camping nights when you're casting around for something fresh and easy to put together. Any white fish will shine in this recipe.

1. Preheat the oven to 450°F. Tear off four 12 x 18-inch sheets of heavy-duty aluminum foil and spray one side of each sheet with nonstick cooking spray.

2. Place a tilapia fillet on top of each foil sheet and sprinkle them equally with the salt, pepper, paprika, if using, and dill.

3. Place 1 or 2 lemon slices on top of each fillet, if you're using them. Drizzle with lemon juice and then top with the tomatoes.

4. To create a packet, bring the long sides of the foil together, then fold twice to create a seal, leaving 1 to 2 inches of room for steam to inflate the packet during cooking. For the two remaining short sides, fold twice to finish sealing.

 Oven

YIELD: 4 SERVINGS

PREP TIME: 10 minutes

COOKING TIME: 15 minutes

Nonstick cooking spray

4 (4- to 6-ounce) tilapia fillets

½ teaspoon salt

½ teaspoon pepper

½ teaspoon paprika (optional)

½ teaspoon dried dill or parsley

Lemon slices, optional

2 lemons, juiced

1 pint cherry tomatoes, halved

5. Place the packets in the oven, seam side up, for 15 minutes. Remove and carefully open the packets. Serve the tilapia in the foil or on a plate, alongside Grilled Zucchini (page 157).

Santa Fe Chicken Packets

The salsa keeps the chicken moist and full of flavor, while the beans and corn round out this traditional Southwestern-flavored packet.

1. Preheat the oven to 425°F. Tear off four 12 x 18-inch pieces of heavy-duty aluminum foil and spray one side of each sheet with nonstick cooking spray.

2. In a large bowl, toss together the chicken, bell pepper, beans, corn, salt, cumin, and pepper.

3. Place an equal amount of the mixture onto the center of each of the four foil sheets. Top each with ¼ cup of salsa.

4. To create a packet, bring the long sides of the foil together, then fold twice to create a seal, leaving 1 to 2 inches of room for steam to inflate the packet during cooking. For the two remaining short sides, fold twice to finish sealing.

5. Place the foil packets in the oven, seam side up, and bake them for 30 minutes. Serve in bowls, topped with sour cream. (This dish goes well with Cilantro Lime Rice, page 162.)

 Oven

YIELD: 4 SERVINGS

PREP TIME: 10 minutes
COOKING TIME: 30 minutes

Nonstick cooking spray

1½ pounds boneless, skinless chicken breasts, cut into 1½-inch pieces

1 red bell pepper, cored, seeded, and cut into 1-inch pieces

1 (15-ounce) can black beans, drained and rinsed

1 (15-ounce) can corn, drained

1 teaspoon salt

1 teaspoon ground cumin

½ teaspoon pepper

1 cup jarred salsa of choice, plus more for serving

Sour cream (optional)

Curry Chicken and Cauliflower Packets

This curry chicken and cauliflower recipe packs a bit of an international flair and is perfect when you're in the mood for something a little different.

1. Preheat the oven to 400°F. Tear off four 12 x 18-inch sheets of heavy-duty aluminum foil and spray one side of each sheet with nonstick cooking spray.

2. Toss together the chicken, cauliflower, and peas. Place an equal amount of the mixture into the center of each foil sheet.

3. In a small bowl, whisk together the coconut milk and curry paste. Drizzle ¼ cup over each mound of chicken mixture. To create a packet, bring the long sides of the foil together, then fold twice to create a seal, leaving 1 to 2 inches of room for steam to inflate the packet during cooking. For the two remaining short sides, fold twice to finish sealing.

4. Place the packets in the oven, seam side up, for 25 minutes. Carefully remove and serve the meal, either in the foil or in bowls with rice. Season with salt and pepper to taste.

 Oven

YIELD: 4 PACKETS

PREP TIME: 10 minutes

COOKING TIME: 25 minutes

Nonstick cooking spray

1½ pounds boneless, skinless chicken breasts, cut into 1½-inch pieces

1 head cauliflower, florets only

1 cup frozen peas, thawed

1 cup coconut milk

2 tablespoons red or green curry paste

Salt and pepper to taste

Garlic Butter Shrimp and Peas Packet

Everyone needs a bit of decadence when they're out on the road, and this shrimp dish will make you feel like you're dining at a five-star restaurant . . . only you'll be seeing a billion stars overhead instead.

1. Preheat the oven to 350°F. Tear off four 12 x 18-inch pieces of heavy-duty aluminum foil and spray one side of each sheet with nonstick cooking spray.

2. In a large bowl, toss together the shrimp, salt, pepper, and garlic.

3. Place an equal amount of the mixture onto the center of each of the four foil sheets. Top each with ¼ cup of the peas and 1 tablespoon of butter.

4. To create a packet, bring the long sides of the foil together, then fold twice to create a seal, leaving 1 to 2 inches of room for steam to inflate the packet during cooking. For the two remaining short sides, fold twice to finish sealing.

5. Place the packets in the oven, seam side up, and bake for 15 minutes. Carefully remove the shrimp mixture and serve it in a bowl with orzo pasta or rice.

 Oven

YIELD: 4 SERVINGS

PREP TIME: 10 minutes

COOKING TIME: 15 minutes

Nonstick cooking spray

1½ pounds raw shrimp, peeled and deveined

1 teaspoon salt

1 teaspoon pepper

2 cloves garlic, finely minced

1 cup frozen peas, thawed

4 tablespoons (½ stick) butter

Chicken, Potato, and Broccoli Foil Packets

This was the first foil packet I developed, and it's still my favorite. Basic ingredients and seasonings make it a popular meal for adults and kids alike.

1. Preheat the oven to 425°F. Tear off four 12 x 18-inch sheets of heavy-duty aluminum foil and spray one side of each sheet with nonstick cooking spray.

2. In a large bowl, combine the chicken, potatoes, onion, and broccoli. Drizzle with the olive oil and toss to coat evenly.

3. In a small bowl, blend the salt, garlic powder, black pepper, and cayenne pepper, if using. Sprinkle the seasoning over the chicken mixture and toss to combine.

4. Place an equal amount of the mixture onto the center of each of the four foil sheets. To create a packet, bring the long sides of the foil together, then fold twice to create a seal, leaving 1 to 2 inches of room for steam to inflate the packet during cooking. For the two

 Oven

YIELD: 4 SERVINGS

PREP TIME: 15 minutes

COOKING TIME: 30 minutes

Nonstick cooking spray

1½ pounds boneless, skinless chicken breasts, cut into 1½-inch cubes

2 red or yellow potatoes, scrubbed and cut into 1-inch cubes

½ medium onion, any kind, cut into ½-inch slivers

2 cups fresh broccoli florets, cut into 1-inch pieces

2 tablespoons extra-virgin olive oil

ingredients continue on following page

remaining short sides, fold twice to finish sealing.

5. Place the packets in the oven, seam side up, and bake for 30 minutes. Carefully remove and open the corner of one packet. Pierce a potato to make sure it is fully cooked. If needed, cook the packets for 10 more minutes.

6. When the vegetables are done to your liking, serve either in the packet or on a plate. Season with additional salt and pepper to taste.

1½ teaspoons salt, plus more to taste

1 teaspoon garlic powder

½ teaspoon black pepper, plus more to taste

¼ teaspoon cayenne pepper (optional)

Sweet and Sour Pork Packets

It's the homemade sweet and sour sauce that makes this recipe a standout. The tender pork soaks up the sauce, but there's just enough to pour over some quick instant rice.

1. Preheat the oven to 400°F. Tear off four 12 x 18-inch sheets of heavy-duty aluminum foil and spray one side of each sheet with nonstick cooking spray.

2. To make the sauce, in a small saucepan over medium-high heat, combine the ketchup, vinegar, brown sugar, soy sauce, and the slurry. Bring the mixture to a boil, whisking constantly. Simmer for 10 minutes, or until the sauce has thickened slightly. Remove it from the heat.

3. Place one-quarter of the pork, peppers, and onion into the center of each sheet of foil.

4. Drizzle the pork mixture with 2 to 3 tablespoons of the sauce. To create a packet, bring the long sides of the foil together, then fold twice to create a seal, leaving 1 to 2 inches of room

 Oven

YIELD: 4 SERVINGS

PREP TIME: 15 minutes

COOKING TIME: 25 minutes

Nonstick cooking spray

¼ cup ketchup

¼ cup white wine vinegar

¼ cup packed brown sugar

1 tablespoon soy sauce

Slurry of 2 tablespoons water and 2 tablespoons cornstarch

1½ pounds pork tenderloin, cut into 1½-inch cubes

1 red bell pepper, cored, seeded, and cut into 1-inch pieces

ingredients continue on following page

for steam to inflate the packet during cooking. For the two remaining short sides, fold twice to finish sealing.

5. Place the packets in the oven, seam side up, and bake for 25 minutes. Carefully remove the packets and serve the sweet and sour pork either in the foil or in bowls with rice.

1 green bell pepper, cored, seeded, and cut into 1-inch pieces

½ medium onion, any kind, cut into 1-inch dice

Grilled Boneless Pork Chops

It's all about the brine. That's how to make grilled pork chops moist and flavorful, so don't skip that step and these chops will quickly make it into your regular rotation. I like to sprinkle them with some yellow peppercorn for a pop of extra color.

1. Pour the salt and sugar into a gallon-size resealable plastic bag and add the water. Seal the bag and shake it to thoroughly combine the salt and sugar. Open the bag and add the 4 pork chops. Seal the bag again and place it in the refrigerator for 1 hour.

2. Preheat the grill to medium-high.

3. Remove the pork chops from the brine and pat them dry. Season the pork chops on both sides with the garlic powder and pepper.

4. Place the chops on the hot grill and close the lid. Cook them for 5 minutes, then flip them. Cook the chops for another 5 minutes. Remove the chops from the grill and let them sit for 5 minutes. The inside should be just slightly pink. (Cook the chops a little longer, if you prefer.)

 Grill

YIELD: 4 SERVINGS

PREP TIME: 5 minutes
COOKING TIME: 10 minutes

¼ cup salt

¼ cup sugar

4 cups water

4 (4- to 5-ounce) boneless pork chops

1 teaspoon garlic powder

½ teaspoon pepper

Grilled Flank Steak

Scoring this cut of beef ¼ inch deep on both sides tenderizes it in no time. Flank steak is best served medium-rare, so be sure to keep an eye on it as it cooks.

1. Preheat the grill to high and close the lid.

2. Keep the steak whole, but use a sharp knife to score it diagonally, about ¼ inch deep, every 2 inches. Slice the meat in the other diagonal direction (it will look like two-inch diamonds across the surface of the steak). Do this to both sides of the steak. Scoring it will allow the seasonings to penetrate and flavor the meat.

3. Rub both sides of the steak with olive oil, then sprinkle both sides with the seasoned salt and pepper. Let the steak rest for 30 minutes before grilling.

4. Put the steak on the grill and close the lid. Let it sit, undisturbed, for 5 minutes. After 5 minutes, flip the steak to the other side and close the lid. Cook the steak for another 5 minutes and then check for doneness.

 Grill

YIELD: 4 SERVINGS

PREP TIME: 35 minutes
COOKING TIME: 10 minutes

1 (1½- to 2-pound) flank steak

1 tablespoon olive oil

2 teaspoons seasoned salt

1 teaspoon pepper

5. The total cooking time is 10 to 12 minutes for a medium-rare to medium steak.

6. Remove the steak from the heat. Let it sit for 5 minutes, then slice the meat diagonally against the grain to make thin slices. Serve the steak immediately or at room temperature. Call it dinner with Summer Veggies Packet, page 153.

Grilled Chicken Quesadillas

I usually make this easy dinner on our travel days, when the trip takes just a little longer than you thought it would, or maybe you're pulling in after dark and everyone is exhausted. These quesadillas are quick, tasty—and *done* in less than fifteen minutes.

1. Preheat the grill to medium-high and close the lid.

2. In a large bowl, mix the chicken, cheese, 1 cup of the salsa, and the onion, until the mixture is well blended.

3. Place two tortillas, opened flat, on the grill and place one-quarter of the chicken mixture onto one half of each tortilla. Fold the other half of the tortilla over the chicken mixture and gently press down with the back of a spatula. Close the grill lid and cook the tortillas for 3 to 4 minutes, until the cheese begins to melt and there are char marks on the bottom of the tortillas. Flip the quesadilla and cook the other side for 2 to 3 minutes. Remove the quesadillas from the grill and slice them into wedges. Use the same method to prepare the remaining tortillas.

 Grill

YIELD: 4 QUESADILLAS

PREP TIME: 5 minutes
COOKING TIME: 10 minutes

2 (12-ounce) cans cooked chicken

2 cups shredded taco blend cheese

1 (15-ounce) jar salsa

½ medium onion, any kind, minced

4 tortillas, burrito size

Toppings: Sour cream, chopped fresh cilantro, diced tomatoes (optional)

4. Top the quesadillas with additional salsa and your choice of other toppings, such as sour cream, cilantro, and diced tomatoes. Serve immediately.

Best Beef Kebabs

Mushrooms and beef are a delightful pair. Add some peppers, onions, and cherry tomatoes to these kebabs and you have a meal fit for a king.

1. In a medium bowl, whisk together the soy sauce, ¼ cup of the olive oil, the vinegar, garlic powder, and black pepper. Add the steak cubes and toss them in the soy sauce mixture to coat them evenly. Let the steak marinate in the refrigerator for 1 hour.

2. Soak eight wooden skewers in water for 30 minutes. It is helpful to double-skewer each kebab to ensure more even cooking. Using wood instead of metal skewers for beef will help prevent overcooking in the middle.

3. Thread the skewers with the steak, mushroom halves, bell pepper pieces, onion slices, and cherry tomatoes, divided equally among the four double-skewered kebabs.

4. Brush the kebabs with the remaining 2 tablespoons of olive oil. Place them on the hot grill and close the lid.

 Grill

YIELD: 4 SERVINGS

PREP TIME: 20 minutes
COOKING TIME: 12 minutes

¼ cup soy sauce

¼ cup plus
2 tablespoons
extra-virgin olive oil

2 tablespoons white
wine vinegar

1 teaspoon garlic powder

½ teaspoon black
pepper

1½ pounds top sirloin
steak, cut into
1½-inch cubes

1 pound whole
mushrooms, scrubbed
and halved

1 large bell pepper, any
color, cored, seeded,
and cut into 1-inch
pieces

*ingredients continue
on following page*

5. Cook the kebabs for 10 to 12 minutes, rotating them two or three times to ensure even cooking. Remove the kebabs with tongs and let them sit for 5 minutes before serving. These kebabs are nice with Ranch Beans (page 149).

1 medium onion, any kind, cut into 1-inch-wide slices

½ pint cherry tomatoes

Easy BBQ Meatball Skewers

Kids love these meatballs and gobble them up. They even eat the vegetables that come with the meatballs! Everything tastes better on a skewer (and it's more fun to eat).

1. Soak eight wooden skewers in water for 30 minutes. Preheat the grill to medium-high.

2. Thread the skewers, alternating the meatballs and bell peppers. Carefully rub oil on the grates of the grill using tongs and a paper towel coated with vegetable oil, then place the skewers on the hot grill. Close the lid.

3. Cook the meatball skewers for 10 to 12 minutes, rotating them every 2 to 3 minutes. Baste the meatballs and peppers with BBQ sauce for the last two rotations.

4. Remove the meatballs when the peppers have cooked to the desired doneness and serve immediately. Goes great with the Easy Coleslaw.

 Grill

YIELD: 4 SERVINGS

PREP TIME: 15 minutes
COOKING TIME: 10 minutes

- 1 (28-ounce) bag fully cooked frozen meatballs, thawed
- 1 green bell pepper, cored, seeded, and cut into 1½-inch pieces
- 1 red bell pepper, cored, seeded, and cut into 1½-inch pieces
- ½ cup favorite BBQ sauce

Red Beans and Rice with Kielbasa

This one-pot pressure cooker meal is economical, flavorful, and gives you lots of leftovers. Using brown rice is essential to the success of this dish.

1. Place the beans, broth, tomatoes with their juice, onion, salt, and garlic powder into the Instant Pot inner pot and mix well. Carefully add the rice to the pot, but do not mix it in (you don't want too much of the rice on the bottom of the pot).

2. Close the lid, ensuring the pressure valve is in the sealing position. Pressure cook on high for 28 minutes.

3. When the cook time is complete, let the pressure cooker naturally release (sit undisturbed) for 10 minutes. Then turn the pressure valve toward the venting position to quick-release the remaining pressure.

4. Carefully remove the lid and stir well. Add the kielbasa slices. Stir the mixture and set the lid back on the pot. Let the pot sit for 5 minutes to allow the kielbasa to warm through. Remove the lid and stir well. The mixture will thicken as it is stirred. Serve in bowls topped with parsley.

 **Instant Pot**

YIELD: 6 SERVINGS

PREP TIME: 5 minutes

COOKING TIME: 30 minutes

TOTAL TIME: 55 minutes
   (including pressure time)

1 cup dried red beans, rinsed

5 cups broth of choice (or 4 cups broth plus 1 cup water)

1 (15-ounce) can fire-roasted diced tomatoes with juice

1 medium onion, any kind, minced

1 teaspoon salt

½ teaspoon garlic powder

1½ cups brown rice, very well rinsed

14 ounces fully cooked Polska kielbasa, sliced crosswise into ½-inch-thick coins

Chopped Italian parsley

Instant Pot Ribs

I am amazed every time I make ribs in my electric pressure cooker—it makes the best, most tender, fall-off-the-bone ribs ever. Be sure to finish them off under the broiler or on the grill to get a perfect char on the outside.

Instant Pot

YIELD: 4 SERVINGS

PREP TIME: 10 minutes
COOKING TIME: 45 minutes
TOTAL TIME: 75 minutes
(including pressure time)

1 slab baby back ribs (about 1½ to 2 pounds)

2 teaspoons salt

2 teaspoons pepper

1 cup apple juice

1 cup **BBQ** sauce, divided

1. Liberally season both sides of the rack of ribs with salt and pepper. Cut it in half if it's too big for your Instant Pot.

2. Pour the apple juice into the inner pot. Place the ribs in the inner pot. Drizzle the ribs with ¼ cup of the BBQ sauce and secure the lid, ensuring the pressure valve is turned toward the sealing position.

3. Pressure cook on high for 25 minutes.

4. When the cook time is complete, let the pressure cooker naturally release (sit undisturbed) for 15 minutes. Then turn the valve to the venting position to quick-release the remaining pressure.

5. Turn on the broiler (or heat your grill) during the 15-minute resting time.

6. Remove the ribs from the pressure cooker and place them on a foil-lined baking sheet. Slather both sides of the ribs with the remaining sauce. Place them under the broiler (or on the grill) for 5 to 10 minutes, watching carefully, to make sure the meat doesn't burn. Remove the ribs from the broiler or grill and brush them with a bit more sauce. Pull them apart and dig in!

SALADS & SIDES

Easy Coleslaw

Summer and coleslaw—you can't have one without the other. Buying bags of mixed shredded cabbage and carrots from the store will save you lots of chopping time, and you can find them almost everywhere. Serve this easy-to-make slaw with all of your favorite summertime sandwiches (like Carolina-Style BBQ Chicken Sandwiches, page 86).

1. Pour the coleslaw mix into a large bowl.

2. In a small bowl, whisk together the mayonnaise, vinegar, sugar, lemon juice, salt, and pepper.

3. Pour the mayonnaise mixture over the coleslaw mix and toss until the slaw is well coated. Refrigerate for 1 hour before serving.

YIELD: 4 SERVINGS

PREP TIME: 5 minutes

COOKING TIME: 0 minutes

1 (14-ounce) bag coleslaw mix of carrots and cabbage

½ cup mayonnaise

3 tablespoons white wine vinegar

2 tablespoons white sugar

1 tablespoon lemon juice

1 teaspoon salt

½ teaspoon white or black pepper

Simple Chopped Green Salad

This is a crisp and refreshing addition to any camping meal. The key to the most delicious, chopped salad is perfectly chilled veggies.

1. In a large bowl mix together the lettuce, tomatoes, carrots, bell pepper, and black olives.

2. In a small bowl, whisk together the oil, vinegar, salt, pepper, Italian seasoning, and garlic powder. Drizzle onto the lettuce mixture.

3. Toss well and top with grated Parmesan cheese, if using. Serve cold.

YIELD: 6 SERVINGS

PREP TIME: 15 minutes
COOKING TIME: 0 minutes

1 head romaine or iceberg lettuce, rinsed and chopped into 1- to 2-inch pieces

2 Roma tomatoes, diced

1 cup baby carrots, cut crosswise into ½-inch coins

1 red bell pepper, cored, seeded, and cut into ½-inch pieces

4 ounces sliced black olives, drained

¼ cup extra-virgin olive oil

¼ cup white wine vinegar

1 teaspoon salt

1 teaspoon pepper

½ teaspoon Italian seasoning

½ teaspoon garlic powder

Cucumber Tomato Salad

Ripe summertime tomatoes transform this salad from good to great. And the splash of flavor from the white wine vinegar and quality olive oil complement the other ingredients flawlessly.

1. Rinse the cucumber and slice off the ends. Peel off alternating strips of the skin lengthwise. The cucumber will look striped, with alternating skin on and off.

2. Slice the cucumber lengthwise in half, and then slice each half lengthwise again. You will have 4 long, full-length cucumber spears. Cut the strips of cucumber crosswise into ½-inch pieces.

3. Place the cucumber and tomatoes into a medium bowl.

4. In a small bowl, whisk together the oil, vinegar, salt, pepper, and basil. Drizzle the dressing over the tomatoes and cucumber. Serve cold or at room temperature.

YIELD: 4 SERVINGS

PREP TIME: 15 minutes
COOKING TIME: 0 minutes

1 medium-size cucumber

2 medium fresh tomatoes, cut into ½-inch pieces

2 tablespoons extra-virgin olive oil

2 tablespoons white wine vinegar

1 teaspoon salt

½ teaspoon pepper

½ teaspoon dried basil

Spinach Salad with Strawberries

Does anything say "summertime" more than fresh strawberries and spinach? This simple but elegant salad will please even the most discerning RVers.

1. In a large bowl, toss together the spinach and strawberries

2. In a small bowl, whisk together the oil, vinegar, salt, and pepper. Drizzle the dressing over the spinach mixture. Toss to combine.

3. Top the dressed spinach mix with walnut pieces and goat cheese. Lightly toss to combine. Serve the salad cold or at room temperature.

YIELD: 4 SERVINGS

PREP TIME: 10 minutes

COOKING TIME: 0 minutes

3 to 4 cups baby spinach, rinsed

1 pint fresh strawberries, washed, stems removed, and sliced

½ cup walnut pieces

4 ounces goat cheese, cut or crumbled

4 tablespoons extra-virgin olive oil

4 tablespoons balsamic vinegar

½ teaspoon salt

½ teaspoon pepper

Fruit Salad

Use the best and freshest fruit you can get for this summer favorite. Don't make more than you can eat, however, because this delightful salad does not keep well.

1. In a large bowl, mix together the watermelon, grapes, blueberries, pineapple, and strawberries.

2. In a small bowl, whisk together the vinegar and sugar. Drizzle the dressing over the fruit mixture and toss to coat.

3. Serve cold or at room temperature.

YIELD: 8 SERVINGS

PREP TIME: 20 minutes

COOKING TIME: 0 minutes

1 small seedless watermelon, cut into 2-inch pieces (about 3-4 pounds)

1 bunch red grapes, halved lengthwise

1 cup fresh or frozen blueberries

1 small pineapple, peeled, cored, and cut into 1-inch pieces

1 pint strawberries, washed, stems removed, and halved lengthwise

2 tablespoons balsamic vinegar

2 tablespoons white sugar

Ranch Beans

I pull out this recipe whenever I'm making Baked Brats with Onions and Peppers (page 67) or Frozen Hamburgers Done Right (page 72). Cans of diced tomatoes and green chillies come in mild and hot flavors. I love the heat they add, but fair warning—the hot version is very hot.

1. Combine the beans, diced tomatoes, paprika, salt, pepper, and cumin in a large saucepan and cook over medium-high heat for 10 minutes, or until the mixture is simmering. Stir in a handful of chopped parsley, if you like, before serving.

2. Serve warm.

 Cooktop

YIELD: 4 SERVINGS

PREP TIME: 5 minutes
COOKING TIME: 10 minutes

2 (15-ounce) cans pinto beans, rinsed and drained

1 (10-ounce) can diced tomatoes and green chilies with juices, mild or hot

1 teaspoon smoked paprika

1 teaspoon salt

½ teaspoon pepper

½ teaspoon ground cumin

Topping: small bunch flat leaf parsley, chopped (optional)

Herbed Baby Potatoes

Fresh herbs really make this potato dish shine, but dried herbs will do in a pinch. Potatoes can handle a fair amount of salt, so don't be shy with it, and you'll have a side dish that goes with almost any entrée you make.

1. Wash the potatoes and place them in a large pot. Fill the pot with water to just above the potatoes. Add the salt and bring the water to a boil. Reduce the heat to medium and simmer the potatoes, partially covered, for 20 minutes.

2. Drain the cooked potatoes and then put them back in the pot. Add the butter and mix until the potatoes are well coated. Add the fresh or dried herbs and mix well.

3. Serve warm.

 Cooktop

YIELD: 4 SERVINGS

PREP TIME: 5 minutes
COOKING TIME: 15 minutes

2 pounds baby potatoes, yellow or red, not peeled

1 tablespoon salt, plus more to taste

2 tablespoons butter

1 tablespoon chopped fresh herbs, such as rosemary, dill, thyme, and Italian parsley (or ½ teaspoon dried rosemary and ½ teaspoon dried thyme)

Pepper to taste

Fresh Green Beans

I probably serve fresh green beans more than any other vegetable, and for good reason—they're healthy and super easy to make. I like beans that have just a little bite, but feel free to cook them longer if you prefer a softer texture.

1. Cut green the beans crosswise into thirds.

2. Heat a large skillet over high heat. Add the oil and butter.

3. When the butter has melted, add the green beans to the skillet and toss them until they're well coated. Let the green beans sit undisturbed for 1 to 2 minutes, until they begin to brown on one side. Stir and let the beans sit for another 30 seconds.

4. Slowly add the water to the green beans (this will create steam). Lower the heat to medium-low and cover the skillet. Steam the green beans for 7–10 minutes, until they're cooked to the desired doneness.

5. Drain any excess water from the beans and sprinkle them with salt. Serve immediately.

 Cooktop

YIELD: 4 SERVINGS

PREP TIME: 5 minutes
COOKING TIME: 15 minutes

1 pound fresh green beans, washed and ends trimmed

1 tablespoon extra-virgin olive oil

1 tablespoon butter

½ cup water

1 teaspoon salt

Summer Veggie Packet

Much like Fruit Salad (page 148), this dish shines best when you use the freshest summer produce you can find. These vegetables are the easiest ones to source in my area, but please use your own favorites.

1. Heat the oven to 400°F. Tear off four 12 x 14-inch sheets of heavy-duty aluminum foil and spray one side of each sheet with nonstick cooking spray.

2. In a large bowl, combine the corn, spinach, zucchini, tomatoes, and mushrooms.

Oven

YIELD: 4 SERVINGS

PREP TIME: 10 minutes

COOKING TIME: 20 minutes

Nonstick cooking spray

2 ears fresh corn, peeled, silk removed, cobs cut in half crosswise

2 cups baby spinach, rinsed

1 medium yellow zucchini, sliced into ½-inch coins

1 medium green zucchini, sliced into ½-inch coins

1 pint cherry or grape tomatoes

½ pound button mushrooms, scrubbed and quartered

ingredients continue on following page

3. In a small bowl, whisk together the oil, lemon juice, salt, pepper, and garlic powder. Drizzle the mixture over the vegetables and toss to combine.

4. Divide the vegetables equally among the sheets of foil, ensuring that each packet gets ½ ear of corn. To create a packet, bring the long sides of the foil together, then fold twice to create a seal, leaving 1 to 2 inches of room for steam to inflate the packet during cooking. For the two remaining short sides, fold twice to finish sealing.

5. Place the packet in the oven, seam side up. Bake for 20 minutes and serve immediately in the foil packet or in bowls.

2 tablespoons extra-virgin olive oil

1 tablespoon lemon juice

1 teaspoon salt

½ teaspoon pepper

½ teaspoon garlic powder

Foil Packet Broccoli on the Grill

This broccoli recipe is the most popular side dish on my blog, and I highly recommend giving it a shot. If you need to save space in your RV fridge, just buy precut broccoli florets.

1. Preheat the grill to medium-high and close the lid.

 Grill

YIELD: 4 SERVINGS

PREP TIME: 5 minutes
COOKING TIME: 20 minutes

2. Tear off one 12 x 18-inch sheet of heavy-duty aluminum foil. Pile the broccoli into the center of the sheet and sprinkle the broccoli with salt.

2 to 3 cups broccoli florets
½ teaspoon salt
½ cup water
1 tablespoon butter

3. Bend up the edges of the foil and pour the water into the center.

4. To create a packet, carefully bring the long sides of the foil together, then fold twice to create a seal, leaving 1 to 2 inches of room for steam to inflate the packet during cooking. For the two remaining short sides, fold twice to finish sealing.

5. Place the packet on the heated grill, seam side up, close the lid, and cook for 15 to 20 minutes. Remove the packet from the grill and open a corner. Pierce a floret with a fork to check for doneness.

6. When the broccoli is done to your taste, pour the water out of the open corner, then open the rest of the packet. Top the broccoli with butter and serve it, either in the packet or on a plate, with your entrée (Meatloaf Muffins, for example, on page 93).

Grilled Zucchini

Grilled zucchini takes almost no time to make but tastes extra special. For the best results, cut the zucchini strips to an even thickness.

1. Preheat the grill to medium-high.

2. Slice the ends off the zucchini. Cut each zucchini lengthwise into four long, thick strips. You should have 8 planks altogether.

3. Drizzle both sides of each strip with olive oil and sprinkle it with salt, Italian seasoning, and pepper.

4. Place the zucchini strips on the hot grill and close the lid. Cook for 6 minutes, flipping the strips halfway through the cooking time.

5. Serve immediately. I like to pair this with Lemon Herb Tilapia Foil Packets (page 120).

 Grill

YIELD: 4 SERVINGS

PREP TIME: 5 minutes

COOKING TIME: 6 minutes

2 large green zucchini

1 tablespoon extra-virgin olive oil

1 teaspoon salt

1 teaspoon Italian seasoning

½ teaspoon pepper

Grilled Vegetable Salad

The extra bit of chopping this recipe takes is well worth it. There's nothing quite like the taste of freshly grilled summertime vegetables when you're enjoying the great outdoors. Don't forget to chill the salad for a couple hours before serving.

1. Preheat the grill to medium-high.

2. Place the zucchini, onion, and tomatoes in a large bowl and toss with 2 tablespoons of the olive oil.

3. Place the vegetables, plus the whole head of romaine lettuce, on the grill, being careful to not let anything slip through the grates. Close the lid and cook for 6 to 8 minutes, rotating all the vegetables halfway through the cooking time. Keep an eye on them and ensure no vegetables get too charred.

4. Remove the vegetables from the grill. Cut the core off the romaine and cut the leaves into large pieces. Place all the vegetables in a large bowl.

5. In a small bowl, whisk together the remaining ¼ cup of olive oil, the white wine vinegar, salt, Italian

 Grill

YIELD: 4 SERVINGS

PREP TIME: 20 minutes
COOKING TIME: 6 minutes

1 large green zucchini, cut lengthwise into strips

1 yellow zucchini, cut lengthwise into strips

1 medium onion, any kind, quartered

2 Roma tomatoes, seeded and quartered

¼ cup plus 2 tablespoons extra-virgin olive oil

1 head romaine lettuce, rinsed, kept whole

¼ cup white wine vinegar

ingredients continue on following page

seasoning, pepper, and garlic powder. Drizzle the dressing over the vegetables and toss to coat them well.

6. Refrigerate the salad for about 2 hours before serving.

7. Season with additional salt and pepper to taste.

1 teaspoon salt, plus more to taste

1 teaspoon Italian seasoning

½ teaspoon pepper, plus more to taste

½ teaspoon garlic powder

Grilled Corn on the Cob

This is one of the best things ever. Period.

1. Preheat the grill to high and close the lid.

2. Peel back the corn husks, but don't remove them. Remove all the cornsilk strands.

3. Pull the husks over the corn and soak them in a large bowl of water for 30 minutes.

4. Remove the corn from the water, pull back the husks, and squeeze out any excess water from the husks. Pat them dry with a paper towel.

5. In a small bowl, mix together the seasoned salt, salt, and pepper. Sprinkle the corn evenly with the seasonings and then cover the corn with the husks again.

6. Place the corn on the hot grill and close the lid. Cook for approximately 12 minutes, rotating the corn every 3 to 4 minutes.

8. Take the corn off the grill. Remove the husks. Smear the corn with butter and serve immediately.

 Grill

YIELD: 4 SERVINGS

PREP TIME: 5 minutes
COOKING TIME: 12 minutes

4 ears corn, in their husks
1 teaspoon seasoned salt
1 teaspoon salt
1 teaspoon pepper
Butter

Cilantro Lime Rice

For a complete meal, whip up a batch of this rice when you're serving Beef Enchilada Bake (page 91) or Southwestern Skillet Dinner (page 103). I like to use parboiled (also known as converted) white rice, but traditional long-grain will work too.

1. Place the rice, water, oil, salt, lime zest, and half of the lime juice into the inner pot of the pressure cooker. Stir the mixture.

2. Secure the lid, ensuring the pressure valve is turned toward the sealing position. Press the Rice function button. The time, pressure, and temperature will be automatically set.

3. When the cook time is complete, quick-release the pressure by turning the valve in the venting position. Carefully remove the lid.

4. Add the remaining lime juice and chopped cilantro to the rice and fluff it with a fork. Serve the rice as a side dish or use it in other dishes that call for cooked rice.

 Instant Pot

YIELD: 4 SERVINGS

PREP TIME: 5 minutes

COOKING TIME: 12 minutes

TOTAL TIME: 25 minutes
(including pressure time)

2 cups white rice, rinsed well to remove the starch

3 cups water

1 tablespoon extra-virgin olive oil

2 teaspoons salt

Juice and zest of 1 lime

1 bunch cilantro, chopped

DESSERTS

No-Bake Mini Cheesecakes

Yes, it's this easy to have cheesecake when you're out RVing. No bake. No mess. Fabulous dessert. Everyone's happy.

FOR THE GRAHAM CRACKER CRUST

1. Place the graham crackers in a gallon-size resealable plastic bag, then use a rolling pin or a mallet to crush into crumbs.

2. Pour the crumbs into a medium bowl. Add the sugar and melted butter and blend well. Spoon one-quarter of the mixture into the bottom of a plastic beverage cup, and repeat with three more beverage cups, packing the crumb mixture firmly into the bottom of each cup (the bottom of a drinking glass or a metal ½-cup measure works well for this) and slightly up the sides. Place the cups in the refrigerator for 15 minutes to firm up the crust.

FOR THE CREAM CHEESE FILLING

1. In a medium bowl, blend the cream cheese (make sure it's at room temperature), sweetened

 Make Ahead

YIELD: 4 SERVINGS

PREP TIME: 20 minutes
COOKING TIME: 0 minutes

GRAHAM CRACKER CRUST

1½ cups crushed graham crackers (about 8 sheets)

¼ cup white sugar

6 tablespoons melted butter

CREAM CHEESE FILLING

8 ounces cream cheese, at room temperature

¾ cup (about 7 ounces) sweetened condensed milk

2 tablespoons lime juice

½ teaspoon vanilla extract

Topping: Fresh blueberries or sliced strawberries (optional)

condensed milk, lime juice, and vanilla extract, using a whisk or handheld mixer.

2. Spoon one-quarter of this mixture into each crust-lined beverage cup. Refrigerate the cups for at least 4 hours or, covered, overnight.

3. Just before serving, top the cheesecakes with a sprinkling of crushed graham crackers, a few fresh blueberries, or some sliced strawberries. Grab a cup and sit by your campfire at dessert time!

Skillet Cake and Berries

Fresh strawberries are my favorite choice for this dessert. They hold up well in the cake and blend perfectly with the chocolate chips if you choose to use them (I would!).

1. Place the berries in a large bowl.

2. In a small bowl, whisk together the sugar and balsamic vinegar. Pour the mixture over the berries and toss until they are well coated. Set the bowl aside.

3. Place a large skillet on the cooktop over medium-high heat. Add the butter to the skillet.

4. When the butter is melted, add the pound cake cubes to the skillet, arranging them in a single layer on the bottom of the pan. Let the pan sit, undisturbed, for 2 to 3 minutes, then flip over the pound cake cubes and let them sit for another 2 to 3 minutes until they're lightly browned on all sides.

 Cooktop

YIELD: 4 SERVINGS

PREP TIME: 15 minutes
COOKING TIME: 5 minutes

2 cups fresh berries of choice, rinsed, and stems removed if necessary

2 tablespoons white sugar

2 tablespoons balsamic vinegar

4 tablespoons butter

1 store-bought pound cake (about 12 ounces), cut into 1-inch cubes

¼ cup milk chocolate chips (optional)

Topping: Canned whipped cream (optional)

5. Remove the pan from the heat and pour the berry mixture over the cake. Sprinkle chocolate chips (if using) over the top. Do not stir them in.

6. Cover the skillet and let it sit undisturbed for 5 minutes or until the berries are warm and the chocolate has melted.

7. Carefully fold the mixture together and serve it in bowls. Top with whipped cream.

Italian Apple Crostata

Pull this recipe out when you want something really fancy but don't want to spend a ton of time in the kitchen. This rustic Italian crostata has all the comforting flavors of a homemade apple pie but takes far less time to make.

1. Preheat the oven to 400°F. Line a baking sheet with parchment paper (or spray with nonstick cooking spray).

2. Roll out the dough according to the directions on the package and place it in the center of the baking sheet.

3. In a large bowl, toss together the apples, flour, 3 tablespoons of the sugar, orange zest, cinnamon, and nutmeg.

4. Mound the apple mixture in the center of the rolled-out dough, leaving about a three-inch margin around the edges.

5. Dot the apple mixture with the pieces of butter. Gently lift and drape the edges over the apples, pleating the dough every 2 to 3 inches to form a circle.

 Oven

YIELD: 4 SERVINGS

PREP TIME: 20 minutes
COOKING TIME: 30 minutes

Nonstick cooking spray

1 refrigerated pie crust

2 cups (approximately 3) large cooking apples (Granny Smith, Fuji, Honey Crisp), cored, peeled, and diced

¼ cup all-purpose flour

3 tablespoons plus ½ tablespoon white sugar

½ teaspoon orange zest

½ teaspoon ground cinnamon

⅛ teaspoon ground nutmeg

3 tablespoons cold butter, cut into ½-inch pieces

6. Sprinkle the edge of the dough with the remaining sugar. Bake the crostata for 25 to 35 minutes, until the apples are soft and the crust is lightly browned.

7. Remove the crostata from the oven and let it rest for 15 minutes before serving.

Apple Pie Packets

This may not be your mama's apple pie, but you'll get to enjoy all the fabulous flavors of the classic dessert with virtually no cleanup.

1. Preheat the oven to 450°F. Tear off four 12 x 18-inch sheets of aluminum foil and spray one side of each sheet with nonstick cooking spray.

2. In a large bowl, mix the apples and lemon juice. Divide the apple mixture among the sheets of foil, mounding it evenly in the center of each sheet.

3. In a small bowl, mix together the cornstarch, brown sugar, white sugar, and cinnamon. Sprinkle it evenly on top of the apple mounds.

4. Divide the pieces of butter equally over the apple mounds, then top with the crushed walnut pieces.

5. To create a packet, bring the long sides of the foil together, then fold twice to create a seal, leaving 1 to 2 inches of room for steam to inflate the packet during cooking. For the two remaining short sides, fold twice to finish sealing.

 Oven

YIELD: 4 SERVINGS

PREP TIME: 15 minutes
COOKING TIME: 15 minutes

Nonstick cooking spray

3 medium-size apples (a mix of Granny Smith and any baking apple, such as Honeycrisp or Gala), cored, peeled, and diced into 1-inch pieces

1 tablespoon lemon juice

1 tablespoon cornstarch

¼ cup packed brown sugar

¼ cup white sugar

2 teaspoons ground cinnamon

2 tablespoons cold butter, cut into small pieces

½ cup crushed walnut pieces

6. Place the packets in the oven, seam side up, for 15 minutes. Remove them from the oven and let them sit for 10 minutes.

7. Carefully open and eat the pie out of the foil packet or put it in a dish and top the pie with ice cream.

Mini Cherry Pies

It's hard to believe that such a delicious dessert can be made with only two ingredients. Here it is! It's also a great dessert to enjoy while sitting by the campfire.

1. Preheat the oven to 375°F.

2. Open the can of biscuits and, using a rolling pin or bottle, flatten each biscuit into a 6-inch circle.

3. Press the biscuit circles into the cups of a muffin pan. There should be enough dough hanging outside the cups so that you can seal them shut when they are filled.

4. Spoon 1 to 2 tablespoons of the cherry pie filling into the center of each dough circle. Bring the edges together to seal the dough shut.

5. Bake the pies for 15 to 18 minutes.

6. Remove the pies from the oven and let them rest for 10 minutes before serving.

 Oven

YIELD: 8 SERVINGS

PREP TIME: 10 minutes
COOKING TIME: 15 minutes

1 (12-ounce) can refrigerated biscuits

1 (21-ounce) can cherry pie filling

Cherry Chocolate Cake

This is another secret recipe from my sister's mother-in-law—the very one who got our entire family into the whole RV-life thing. It's a big hit at camping potluck parties.

FOR THE CAKE

1. Preheat the oven to 350°F. Spray a 9 x 13-inch baking pan with nonstick cooking spray. (Be sure the pan fits in your RV oven.)

2. In a large bowl, combine the cake mix, cherry pie filling, egg, and almond extract, if using, and stir until smooth.

3. Pour the batter into the prepared pan and bake for 25 to 30 minutes.

FOR THE FROSTING

1. In a small saucepan, combine the sugar, butter, and milk over medium-high heat.

2. Bring the mixture to a boil for 1 minute, stirring constantly. Remove the pan from heat, add the chocolate chips, and stir until smooth.

3. Pour the frosting over the warm cake. Serve warm or at room temperature.

 Oven

YIELD: 8 SERVINGS

PREP TIME: 10 minutes

COOKING TIME: 30 minutes

CHERRY CHOCOLATE CAKE

Nonstick cooking spray

1 box chocolate cake mix

1 (21-ounce) can cherry pie filling

1 egg, beaten

1 teaspoon almond extract (optional)

CHOCOLATE FROSTING (OR USE STORE-BOUGHT FROSTING)

1 cup white sugar

5 tablespoons butter

⅓ cup whole milk

6 ounces semi-sweet chocolate chips

Blueberry Crumble

Picking fresh blueberries is very popular in many parts of the country when people are out and enjoying our beautiful outdoors. If you're lucky enough to be in one of those areas, this is the dish to highlight those plump and sweet fresh berries.

1. Preheat the oven to 375°F. Spray an 8 x 8-inch baking pan with nonstick cooking spray.

2. In a medium bowl, mix together the blueberries, sugar, lemon juice, cornstarch, and vanilla. Pour the mixture into the prepared baking pan.

3. To make the topping, in a medium bowl mix together the oats, flour, brown sugar, cinnamon, and salt. Using two knives, cut in the cold, cubed butter until the mixture is crumbly.

4. Pour the topping over the blueberry mixture and spread it evenly over the surface.

 Oven

YIELD: 6 SERVINGS

PREP TIME: 15 minutes
COOKING TIME: 40 minutes

Nonstick cooking spray

4 cups fresh blueberries

2 tablespoons white sugar

1 tablespoon lemon juice

1 tablespoon cornstarch

1 teaspoon vanilla extract

ingredients continue on following page

5. Bake the crumble for 40 minutes. Let it rest for 10 minutes before serving. Serve with a dollop of whipped cream and garnish with a sprig of fresh mint if you have it on hand. Of course, this crumble is delicious without any embellishments!

OAT TOPPING

1 cup rolled oats

¾ cup all-purpose flour

½ cup packed brown sugar

½ teaspoon ground cinnamon

¼ teaspoon salt

1 stick cold butter, cut into small cubes

S'mores Bake

Toasting marshmallows over an open campfire is a long-standing tradition, but when you can't build a fire, these baked s'mores are just as tasty (and a lot less messy!).

1. Preheat the oven to 350°F. Spray the bottom of an 8 x 8-inch baking pan with nonstick cooking spray and place nine of the graham cracker squares in the bottom of the pan, in a single layer.

2. Spread half of the marshmallows on top of the graham crackers. Top the marshmallows with all of the chocolate chips.

3. Place the remaining nine graham cracker squares on top of the chocolate chips, then top them with the remaining half of the marshmallows.

4. Bake the s'mores for 10 minutes or until the marshmallows are golden brown. Serve warm.

 Oven

YIELD: 6 SERVINGS

PREP TIME: 15 minutes
COOKING TIME: 10 minutes

Nonstick cooking spray

1 sleeve graham crackers (about 9 crackers), halved

2 to 3 cups miniature marshmallows

1 cup milk chocolate chips

Peanut Butter Chocolate Banana Boat

You'll feel like a kid again when you eat one of these. Add a dollop of whipped cream if you really want to hearken back to childhood.

1. Preheat the grill to medium.

2. Slice each unpeeled banana lengthwise, down the concave side of the banana. Do not cut through the back peel.

3. Spread 1 tablespoon of peanut butter into the opening in each banana. Top the peanut butter with ¼ of the chocolate chips, pressing the chips gently into the opening.

4. Press the bananas closed a bit, then wrap them tightly in aluminum foil.

5. Place the foil-wrapped bananas on the grill and close the lid. Cook for 10 minutes or until the chocolate is melted. Serve the bananas with a spoon and eat them directly out of the peel.

 Grill

YIELD: 4 SERVINGS

PREP TIME: 10 minutes
COOKING TIME: 10 minutes

4 bananas, unpeeled

4 tablespoons peanut butter

1 cup milk chocolate chips or a chopped chocolate bar

Grilled Glazed Pineapple Spears

The intense heat of the grill turns these cool, sweet, fresh pineapple spears into a rich, golden treat that complements any camping meal.

1. Preheat the grill to medium and close the lid.

2. In a small bowl, whisk together the melted butter, brown sugar, cinnamon, cayenne pepper, and bourbon (if using).

3. Place the pineapple spears on a large plate and brush them with the butter mixture on all sides.

4. Place the pineapple on the grill and cook the spears for 8 to 10 minutes, turning them occasionally to prevent burning.

5. Serve the warm pineapple spears with a dollop of whipped cream.

 Grill

YIELD: 4 SERVINGS

PREP TIME: 15 minutes
COOKING TIME: 10 minutes

½ cup (1 stick) butter, melted

½ cup packed brown sugar

1 teaspoon ground cinnamon

¼ teaspoon cayenne pepper

2 tablespoons bourbon (optional, but really good)

1 pineapple, peeled, cored, and cut into spears

Whipped cream

DRINKS

Coffee—Three Options

I've made coffee pretty much every way possible over the course of my camping years. And while there are numerous ways to do it, here are the methods we use the most.

DRIP

1. Place a coffee filter into the drip machine coffee basket and add the ground coffee.

2. Pour the water into the water reservoir and place the carafe on the warming plate.

3. Press the Start button and wait until the coffee is fully brewed.

4. Enjoy with your favorite additions such as sugar or creamer.

YIELD: 4 CUPS

PREP TIME: up to 5 minutes

COOKING TIME: up to 10 minutes

DRIP

8 tablespoons ground coffee

8 cups water

POUR OVER

1. Line the funnel of the pour-over pot with a coffee filter and place the ground coffee in the funnel. Place the funnel over the pour-over pot.

2. Slowly pour the hot water over the grounds, approximately 1 cup at a time, and let it drain into the pour-over pot.

3. Repeat until all the water is used. Serve the coffee in warm mugs.

POUR OVER

8 tablespoons ground coffee

6 to 8 cups hot water

COFFEE PRESS (FRENCH PRESS)

1. Place the ground coffee into the bottom of the carafe. Slowly pour the hot water—not quite boiling—into the carafe and gently stir.

2. Insert the plunger into the top of the carafe but do not plunge yet.

3. Let the coffee steep for about 4 minutes and then press the plunger very slowly until it goes down as far as it can.

4. Pour the coffee from the carafe immediately. Enjoy black or with your favorite additions.

COFFEE PRESS (FRENCH PRESS)

8 tablespoons coarsely ground coffee (must be very coarse)

8 cups very hot water

Classic Easy Bloody Mary

Camping isn't camping without enjoying the occasional Bloody Mary. (Well, at least not for us!) Using a premade mix is the easy way to make the drink, but you can also make your own and flavor it any way you like.

1. Fill two glasses with ice.

2. Divide the Bloody Mary mix among the glasses and pour over the ice.

3. Add 2 ounces of vodka to each glass. Add a squeeze of fresh lime juice and a couple dashes of hot sauce.

4. Give each glass a good stir, sit back, and enjoy your morning—or afternoon!

YIELD: 2 DRINKS

PREP TIME: 2 minutes

COOKING TIME: 0 minutes

Ice

16 ounces Bloody Mary mix (we like Mr & Mrs T® Bold & Spicy Bloody Mary Mix)

4 ounces vodka

1 lime, half for juice and half for garnish

4 dashes of your favorite hot sauce

Bourbon Spiked Hot Cocoa

You can leave the bourbon out of this one if you'd like, but why would you?

1. Place a medium saucepan on the cooktop over medium heat. Add the milk and bring it to a slight simmer.

2. Whisk the chocolate chips and cocoa powder into the warm milk and bring the mixture to a simmer, whisking constantly.

3. Remove the pan from the heat and add the bourbon.

4. Divide the cocoa into a couple of mugs or heatproof drinking glasses and top with mini marshmallows. Enjoy.

YIELD: 2 DRINKS

PREP TIME: 5 minutes
COOKING TIME: 5 minutes

3 cups whole milk

1 cup milk chocolate chips

¼ cup cocoa powder

3 ounces bourbon

Topping: ½ cup mini marshmallows (optional)

Jack and Coke

This drink is basic and simple. And always a favorite. We opt for Caffeine-Free Coca-Cola in the evenings, but any kind of cola will do at any time of day.

1. Fill two glasses with ice.

2. Pour 6 ounces (half the can) of cola into each glass.

3. Add 1½ ounces of whiskey to each glass and stir well. Sip and enjoy.

YIELD: 2 DRINKS

PREP TIME: 2 minutes
COOKING TIME: 0 minutes

Ice

1 (12-ounce) can of Coke®, Diet Coke®, or Coke® Zero Sugar

3 ounces Jack Daniel's® Tennessee Whiskey

The Frodka

I was a bit skeptical when I was first introduced to this interesting mix of grapefruit soda and vodka, but one sip was all it took to banish any doubt. It's a great drink to enjoy on a hot summer afternoon.

1. Fill two glasses with ice.

2. Add the soda and vodka to the glass and use a spoon to mix the drink.

3. Garnish with a slice of lime and enjoy.

YIELD: 2 DRINKS

PREP TIME: 2 minutes
COOKING TIME: 0 minutes

Ice
8 ounces Fresca® grapefruit soda
3 ounces vodka
2 lime slices

Dark and Stormy

The spicy, tangy, herby taste of ginger beer pairs perfectly with dark rum to make a fun and different camping cocktail. And since ginger is actually good for you, dare I call this beverage healthy? Yep. I'm going with healthy.

1. Fill two tall, slender glasses with ice. Pour enough ginger beer to fill two-thirds of each glass. Slowly pour the rum over the ginger beer. Garnish the drinks with a lime wedge and serve.

YIELD: 2 DRINKS

PREP TIME: 2 minutes
COOKING TIME: 0 minutes

Ice
12 ounces ginger beer
3 ounces dark rum
2 lime wedges

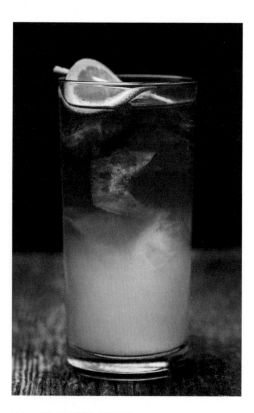

Whiskey on the Rocks

Yes, I'm well aware this is not exactly a recipe. But it's the perfect opportunity to give those jumbo ice cubes mentioned on page 18 a try! Plus, sipping on whiskey by a crackling campfire underneath the stars is about as "camping" as camping gets.

1. Place one ice cube into each of two short glasses or cups.

2. Pour 2 ounces of whiskey into each glass or cup. Sip while enjoying an evening campfire.

YIELD: 2 DRINKS

PREP TIME: 1 minute

COOKING TIME: 0 minutes

4 ounces high-quality whiskey of choice

2 large ice cubes

Hot White Russian Cocktail

Coffee, Kahlúa, vodka, and warm cream? Yes, please! This coffee cocktail will quickly become a favorite.

1. Pour 5 ounces of hot coffee into each of two cups. Add 1½ ounces (one shot) of Kahlúa or other coffee liqueur and ¾ ounce vodka (half a shot) to each cup.

2. Warm 3 ounces of cream over low heat for just a couple of minutes, using whatever heating source you have (stove, camp stove, or campfire). Just keep an eye on the cream because it will scald quickly.

3. As soon as it is warm, add 1½ ounces of cream to each cup of the coffee mixture. Stir and enjoy!

YIELD: 2 DRINKS

PREP TIME: 5 minutes
COOKING TIME: 10 minutes

10 ounces hot coffee
3 ounces Kahlúa
1½ ounces vodka
3 ounces heavy cream

Hot Toddy

I can't promise this toddy will cure a cold, but it's really worth a try when you're nursing a bit of a scratchy throat.

1. In a heatproof pitcher or other container, combine the hot water, whiskey, honey, and lemon juice and stir well.
2. Pour the toddy into two warm mugs.
3. Garnish with a lemon wheel and cinnamon stick, if using. Serve the toddy piping hot.

YIELD: 2 DRINKS

PREP TIME: 5 MINUTES

COOKING TIME: 5 minutes

2 cups hot water

3 ounces whiskey of choice

4 teaspoons honey

2 teaspoons lemon juice

2 lemon wheels (optional)

2 cinnamon sticks (optional)

Conversion Charts

METRIC EQUIVALENTS FOR DIFFERENT TYPES OF INGREDIENTS

Standard Cup	Fine Powder	Grain	Granular	Liquid Solids	Liquid
¾	105 g	113 g	143 g	150 g	180 ml
⅔	93 g	100 g	125 g	133 g	160 ml
½	70 g	75 g	95 g	100 g	120 ml
⅓	47 g	50 g	63 g	67 g	80 ml
¼	35 g	38 g	48 g	50 g	60 ml
⅛	18 g	19 g	24 g	25 g	30 ml

USEFUL EQUIVALENTS FOR LIQUID INGREDIENTS BY VOLUME

¼ tsp	=							1 ml
½ tsp	=							2 ml
1 tsp	=							5 ml
3 tsp	=	1 tbsp	=			½ oz	=	15 ml
		2 tbsp	=	⅛ cup	=	1 oz	=	30 ml
		4 tbsp	=	¼ cup	=	2 oz	=	60 ml
		5 1/8 tbsp	=	⅓ cup	=	3 oz	=	80 ml
		8 tbsp	=	½ cup	=	4 oz	=	120 ml
		10 2/8 tbsp	=	⅔ cup	=	5 oz	=	160 ml
		12 tbsp	=	¾ cup	=	6 oz	=	180 ml
		16 tbsp	=	1 cup	=	8 oz	=	240 ml
		1 pt	=	2 cups	=	16 oz	=	480 ml
		1 qt	=	4 cups	=	32 oz	=	960 ml
						33 oz	=	1000 ml = 1 L

USEFUL EQUIVALENTS FOR DRY INGREDIENTS BY WEIGHT

(To convert ounces to grams, multiply the number of ounces by 30.)

1 oz	=	1/16 lb	=	28.3 g
4 oz	=	¼ lb	=	113 g
8 oz	=	½ lb	=	227 g
12 oz	=	¾ lb	=	340 g
16 oz	=	1 lb	=	454 g

About the Author

HEATHER SCHLUETER, J.D., is an attorney turned CEO turned food blogger and author. She loves cooking for her immediate and extended family, often including anywhere from eight to twenty people, six nights per week.

Heather believes that mealtime is a time for love, laughter, happiness, and bonding. And this is especially true when out RVing with family and friends while enjoying our beautiful country. It's a belief that drives her passion for serving home-cooked, fresh, and comforting family meals. Her love of writing and communication is the foundation on which she has built her successful professional career. Her blog, *The Spicy Apron*, combines her passion for cooking and writing in one place. Heather has crafted her cooking style and built her blog around the motto "Keep it simple. Keep it tasty. Keep it easy to clean." She is passionate about sharing her years of cooking knowledge with others to help them make mealtime an easy, fun, and enjoyable experience.

Heather lives in Scottsdale, Arizona, with her husband, their eight children (although several are grown and out of the house), and their goldendoodle, Bentley. To find out more about Heather, visit www. TheSpicyApron.com and *The Spicy Apron Cooking Show* YouTube channel. Also check out Heather's other cookbooks, *The Instant Pot® Holiday Cookbook* and *Cooking with Your Instant Pot® Mini*, available from your favorite bookseller and online.

Index

A

Alcohol. *See* Drinks
Almonds. *See* Nuts and seeds
Apples
    Apple Pie Packets, 170–171
    Italian Apple Crostata,
        168–169
Appliances
    deciding on "must-haves,"
        15–16
    power considerations, 14–16
    storage considerations and,
        16–21

B

Bacon
    BLT Sandwiches, 59
    Loaded Baked Potato
        Casserole, 96–97
    Oven-Baked Bacon, 43
    recipes with toppings of,
        34–35, 82–83, 114–115
    Tater Tot Breakfast
        Casserole, 48–49
Baked Brats with Onions and
    Peppers, 67
Baked Mostaccioli, 101–102
Banana boat, peanut butter
    chocolate, 179
Basic Baked Chicken Thighs,
    111
Basic Hard-Boiled Eggs, 52
Battery and power
    considerations, 14–16
Beans
    Fresh Green Beans, 152
    other recipes with, 91–92,
        122
    Ranch Beans, 149
    Red Beans and Rice with
        Kielbasa, 139

Southwestern Skillet
    Dinner, 103
Stovetop Chili, 64–65
Beef
    Beef and Tomato Skewers,
        79
    Beef Enchilada Bake,
        91–92
    Best Beef Kebabs, 136–137
    Classic Corned Beef Hash
        Breakfast, 38–39
    Easy BBQ Meatball
        Skewers, 138
    Frozen Hamburgers Done
        Right, 72–73
    Grilled Flank Steak,
        132–133
    Meatloaf Muffins, 93–95
    One-Pot Spaghetti, 107
    Quick Philly Cheesesteak
        Sandwiches, 80–81
    Sheet Pan Steak Fajitas,
        108–109
    Sloppy Joes, 62–63
    Southwestern Skillet
        Dinner, 103
    Stovetop Chili, 64–65
    Stuffed Baked Potatoes,
        114–115
Berries
    Blueberry Crumble,
        174–175
    Fruit Salad, 148
    Skillet Cake and Berries,
        166–167
    Spinach Salad with
        Strawberries, 146–147
    Vanilla Cream Steel Cut
        Oatmeal with Berries, 51
    Yogurt and Berry Parfait, 25
Best Beef Kebabs, 136–137

Beverages. *See* Drinks
Bloody Mary, classic, 184
BLT Sandwiches, 59
Blueberries. *See* Berries
Bourbon Spiked Hot Cocoa,
    185
Brats, baked with onions and
    peppers, 67
Bread and such. *See also*
    Sandwiches and wraps
    French Toast, 41
    Sausage Gravy and
        Biscuits, 42
    Toast—Four Options
        (of toasting methods),
        26–27
Breakfast, 23–52
    Basic Hard-Boiled Eggs, 52
    Breakfast Frittata, 45
    Breakfast Scramble, 37
    Classic Corned Beef Hash
        Breakfast, 38–39
    French Toast, 41
    Make-Ahead Breakfast
        Burritos, 28–29
    Make-Ahead Breakfast
        "Quiche," 32–33
    Make-Ahead Egg Muffin
        Sandwiches, 30–31
    Make-Ahead Pressure
        Cooker Egg Bites, 34–35
    Oven-Baked Bacon, 43
    Perfect Scrambled Eggs, 36
    Sausage Gravy and
        Biscuits, 42
    Sheet Pan Chicken and
        Waffles, 46–47
    Tater Tot Breakfast
        Casserole, 48–49
    Toast—Four Options (of
        toasting methods), 26–27

Vanilla Cream Steel Cut
    Oatmeal with Berries, 51
Yogurt and Berry Parfait,
    25
Broccoli
    Chicken, Potato, and
        Broccoli Foil Packets,
        126–127
    Foil Packet Broccoli on the
        Grill, 155–156
    Loaded Baked Potato
        Casserole, 96–97
    Loaded Potato Soup, 82–83
    Stuffed Baked Potatoes,
        114–115
Burgers. See Sandwiches and
    wraps
Burritos, make-ahead
    breakfast, 28–29

C
Cabbage, Easy Coleslaw, 143
Caprese Chicken, 112–113
Carolina-Style BBQ Chicken
    Sandwiches, 86–87
Casseroles. See also
    Southwestern Skillet
    Dinner
    Loaded Baked Potato
        Casserole, 96–97
    Tater Tot Breakfast
        Casserole, 48–49
Cauliflower and curry chicken
    packets, 123
Charcuterie Board, 56–57
Cheese
    Baked Mostaccioli, 101–102
    Charcuterie Board, 56–57
    eggs with (See Eggs)
    Grilled Chicken
        Quesadillas, 134–135
    Ham Rolls, 58
    Loaded Potato Soup, 82–83
    No-Bake Mini
        Cheesecakes, 164–165
    salads with (See Salads)
    sandwiches with (See
        Sandwiches and wraps)
Cherries
    Cherry Chocolate Cake,
        173

Mini Cherry Pies, 172
Chicken
    Basic Baked Chicken
        Thighs, 111
    Caprese Chicken, 112–113
    Carolina-Style BBQ
        Chicken Sandwiches,
        86–87
    Chicken, Potato, and
        Broccoli Foil Packets,
        126–127
    Crispy Oven-Baked Wings,
        68–69
    Curry Chicken and
        Cauliflower Packets, 123
    Grilled BBQ Chicken
        Drumsticks and Thighs,
        76–77
    Grilled Chicken
        Quesadillas, 134–135
    Grilled Chicken Tender
        Sandwiches, 74
    Hawaiian Chicken
        Skewers, 71
    Loaded Baked Potato
        Casserole, 96–97
    Orzo and Chicken Medley,
        104–105
    Santa Fe Chicken Packets,
        122
    Sheet Pan Chicken and
        Waffles, 46–47
    Sheet Pan Chicken Tenders
        and Veggies, 110
    Shredded Chicken Gyros,
        84–85
    Shredded Chicken Tacos,
        60–61
Chili Cheese Dogs, 75
Chili, stovetop, 64–65
Chocolate
    Bourbon Spiked Hot
        Cocoa, 185
    Cherry Chocolate Cake, 173
    No-Bake Protein Balls, 55
    Peanut Butter Chocolate
        Banana Boat, 179
    S'mores Bake, 177
Cilantro Lime Rice, 162
Classic Corned Beef Hash
    Breakfast, 38–39

Classic Easy Bloody Mary, 184
Cocoa, bourbon spiked hot, 185
Coffee, 15, 16, 22, 182–183
Coke, Jack and, 186
Coleslaw, easy, 143
Condiments to stock, 3
Cooling/freezing food
    about: preparation and
        loading tips, 17–18
    cooler options and
        considerations, 19–21
    ice and, 18–19
    refrigerator/freezer
        considerations, 17–19
Corn
    Grilled Corn on the Cob,
        161
    other recipes with, 103, 122
    Summer Veggie Packet,
        153–154
Corned beef hash breakfast,
    38–39
Crispy Oven-Baked Wings,
    68–69
Cucumber Tomato Salad, 145
Curry Chicken and
    Cauliflower Packets, 123

D
Dark and Stormy, 188
Desserts, 163–180
    Apple Pie Packets, 170–171
    Blueberry Crumble,
        174–175
    Cherry Chocolate Cake, 173
    Grilled Glazed Pineapple
        Spears, 180
    Italian Apple Crostata,
        168–169
    Mini Cherry Pies, 172
    No-Bake Mini
        Cheesecakes, 164–165
    Peanut Butter Chocolate
        Banana Boat, 179
    Skillet Cake and Berries,
        166–167
    S'mores Bake, 177
Dinner, 90–141
    Baked Mostaccioli, 101–102
    Basic Baked Chicken
        Thighs, 111

Dinner (*continued*)
Beef Enchilada Bake, 91–92
Best Beef Kebabs, 136–137
Caprese Chicken, 112–113
Chicken, Potato, and
Broccoli Foil Packets,
126–127
Curry Chicken and
Cauliflower Packets, 123
Easy BBQ Meatball
Skewers, 138
Foil Packet Kielbasa with
Potatoes and Peppers,
118–119
Garlic Butter Shrimp and
Peas Packet with, 125
Grilled Boneless Pork
Chops, 131
Grilled Chicken
Quesadillas, 134–135
Grilled Flank Steak,
132–133
Instant Pot Ribs, 140–141
Lemon Herb Tilapia Foil
Packet, 120–121
Loaded Baked Potato
Casserole, 96–97
Meatloaf Muffins, 93–95
One-Pot Creamy Sausage
and Rice, 106
One-Pot Spaghetti, 107
Orzo and Chicken Medley,
104–105
Red Beans and Rice with
Kielbasa, 139
Santa Fe Chicken Packets,
122
Sheet Pan Chicken
Tenders and Veggies, 110
Sheet Pan Steak Fajitas,
108–109
Shepherd's Pie,
Thanksgiving Style,
98–100
Southwestern Skillet
Dinner, 103
Spicy Andouille Sausage
and Red Potatoes
Packet, 116–117
Stuffed Baked Potatoes,
114–115

Sweet and Sour Pork
Packets, 128–129
Dishes, washing, 22
Dogs, chili cheese, 75
Drinks, 181–191
about: coffee preparation
considerations, 15, 16,
22, 182–183; water
considerations and,
21–22
Bourbon Spiked Hot
Cocoa, 185
Classic Easy Bloody Mary,
184
Coffee—Three Options,
182–183
Dark and Stormy, 188
The Frodka, 187
Hot Toddy, 191
Hot White Russian
Cocktail, 190
Jack and Coke, 186
Whiskey on the Rocks, 189

E

Easy BBQ Meatball Skewers,
138
Easy Coleslaw, 143
Eggs
Basic Hard-Boiled Eggs, 52
Breakfast Frittata, 45
Breakfast Scramble, 37
French Toast, 41
Make-Ahead Breakfast
Burritos, 28–29
Make-Ahead Breakfast
"Quiche," 32–33
Make-Ahead Egg Muffin
Sandwiches, 30–31
Make-Ahead Pressure
Cooker Egg Bites, 34–35
Perfect Scrambled Eggs, 36
Tater Tot Breakfast
Casserole, 48–49
Electrical power
considerations, 14–16
Enchilada bake, beef, 91–92

F

Fajitas, sheet pan, 108–109
Fish and seafood

Garlic Butter Shrimp and
Peas Packet with, 125
Lemon Herb Tilapia Foil
Packet, 120–121
Foil packets
Apple Pie Packets, 170–171
Chicken, Potato, and
Broccoli Foil Packets,
126–127
Curry Chicken and
Cauliflower Packets, 123
Foil Packet Broccoli on the
Grill, 155
Foil Packet Kielbasa with
Potatoes and Peppers,
118–119
Garlic Butter Shrimp and
Peas Packet with, 125
Lemon Herb Tilapia Foil
Packet, 120–121
Santa Fe Chicken Packets,
122
Spicy Andouille Sausage
and Red Potatoes
Packet, 116–117
Summer Veggie Packet,
153–154
Sweet and Sour Pork
Packets, 128–129
French Toast, 41
Fresh Green Beans, 152
Frittata, breakfast, 45
The Frodka, 187
Frozen Hamburgers Done
Right, 72–73
Fruit Salad, 148

G

Garlic Butter Shrimp and
Peas Packet, 125
Graham cracker crust. *See* No-
Bake Mini Cheesecakes
Graham crackers, in S'mores
Bake, 177
Grapes, in Fruit Salad, 148
Gravy and biscuits, sausage,
42
Green beans, fresh, 152
Grilled BBQ Chicken
Drumsticks and Thighs,
76–77

Grilled Boneless Pork Chops, 131
Grilled Chicken Quesadillas, 134–135
Grilled Chicken Tender Sandwiches, 74
Grilled Corn on the Cob, 161
Grilled Flank Steak, 132–133
Grilled Glazed Pineapple Spears, 180
Grilled Vegetable Salad, 158–159
Grilled Zucchini, 157
Gyros, shredded chicken, 84–85

H
Ham
    Breakfast Frittata, 45
    Charcuterie Board, 56–57
    Ham Rolls, 58
    Make-Ahead Egg Muffin Sandwiches, 30–31
Hard-boiled eggs, 52
Hash, classic corned beef breakfast, 38–39
Hawaiian Chicken Skewers, 71
Herbed Baby Potatoes, 151
Hot dogs, chili cheese, 75
Hot Toddy, 191
Hot White Russian Cocktail, 190

I
Ice, 18–19
Instant Pot Ribs, 140–141
Italian Apple Crostata, 168–169

J
Jack and Coke, 186

K
Kebabs. *See* Skewers
Kielbasa. *See* Sausage
Kitchen
    organizing staples, 2–3
    pantry staples, 2–3

L
Lemon Herb Tilapia Foil Packet, 120–121
Lettuce wraps, turkey, 66

Loaded Baked Potato Casserole, 96–97
Loaded Potato Soup, 82–83
Lunch and snacks, 53–89
    Baked Brats with Onions and Peppers, 67
    Beef and Tomato Skewers, 79
    BLT Sandwiches, 59
    Carolina-Style BBQ Chicken Sandwiches, 86–87
    Charcuterie Board, 56–57
    Chili Cheese Dogs, 75
    Crispy Oven-Baked Wings, 68–69
    Frozen Hamburgers Done Right, 72–73
    Grilled BBQ Chicken Drumsticks and Thighs, 76–77
    Grilled Chicken Tender Sandwiches, 74
    Ham Rolls, 58
    Hawaiian Chicken Skewers, 71
    Loaded Potato Soup, 82–83
    No-Bake Protein Balls, 55
    Pulled Pork Pizza, 88–89
    Quick Philly Cheesesteak Sandwiches, 80–81
    Shredded Chicken Gyros, 84–85
    Shredded Chicken Tacos, 60–61
    Sloppy Joes, 62–63
    Stovetop Chili, 64–65
    Turkey Lettuce Wraps, 66

M
Make-Ahead Breakfast Burritos, 28–29
Make-Ahead Breakfast "Quiche," 32–33
Make-Ahead Egg Muffin Sandwiches, 30–31
Make-Ahead Pressure Cooker Egg Bites, 34–35
Meal planning
    about: overview and keys to success, 6–7

sample plan (long weekend), 8
sample plan (two weeks), 9–11
template, 12–14
Meal prep
    about: resource management overview, 14
    power considerations, 14–16
    storage considerations, 16
Measurement conversion charts, 192
Meatball skewers, BBQ, 138
Meatloaf Muffins, 93–95
Mini Cherry Pies, 172
Mostaccioli, baked, 101–102
Mushrooms, 45, 136–137, 153–154

N
No-Bake Mini Cheesecakes, 164–165
No-Bake Protein Balls, 55
Nuts and seeds
    Charcuterie Board, 56–57
    No-Bake Protein Balls, 55
    Peanut Butter Chocolate Banana Boat, 179

O
Oats
    Blueberry Crumble, 174–175
    No-Bake Protein Balls, 55
    Vanilla Cream Steel Cut Oatmeal with Berries, 51
Oils, 3
One-Pot Creamy Sausage and Rice, 106
One-Pot Spaghetti, 107
Organizing pantry items, 3–4
Orzo and Chicken Medley, 104–105
Oven-Baked Bacon, 43

P
Packets. *See* Foil packets
Pantry, organizing, 3–4
Pantry, staples, 2–3

Parfait, yogurt and berry, 25
Pasta
    Baked Mostaccioli, 101–102
    Garlic Butter Shrimp and
        Peas Packet with, 125
    One-Pot Spaghetti, 107
    Orzo and Chicken Medley,
        104–105
    Sheet Pan Chicken
        Tenders and Veggies
        with, 110
Peanut butter. *See* Nuts and
    seeds
Peas, garlic butter shrimp
    and, 125
Peppers
    Baked Brats with Onions
        and Peppers, 87
    Foil Packet Kielbasa with
        Potatoes and Peppers,
        118–119
    other recipes with, 45, 71,
        108–109, 128–129, 138
Perfect Scrambled Eggs, 36
Philly cheesesteak
    sandwiches, 80–81
Pineapple
    Fruit Salad, 148
    Grilled Glazed Pineapple
        Spears, 180
    other recipes with, 71,
        88–89
Pizza, pulled pork, 88–89
Pork. *See also* Bacon; Ham;
    Sausage
    Grilled Boneless Pork
        Chops, 131
    Instant Pot Ribs, 140–141
    Pulled Pork Pizza, 88–89
    Sweet and Sour Pork
        Packets, 128–129
Potatoes
    Chicken, Potato, and
        Broccoli Foil Packets,
        126–127
    Foil Packet Kielbasa with
        Potatoes and Peppers,
        118–119
    Herbed Baby Potatoes, 151
    Loaded Baked Potato
        Casserole, 96–97

Loaded Potato Soup, 82–83
    Make-Ahead Breakfast
        Burritos, 28–29
    Make-Ahead Breakfast
        "Quiche," 32–33
    Spicy Andouille Sausage
        and Red Potatoes
        Packet, 116–117
    Tater Tot Breakfast
        Casserole, 48–49
Power considerations, 14–16
Protein balls, no-bake, 55
Pulled Pork Pizza, 88–89

Q
Quesadillas, grilled chicken,
    134–135
"Quiche," make-ahead, 32–33
Quick Philly Cheesesteak
    Sandwiches, 80–81

R
Ranch Beans, 149
Red Beans and Rice with
    Kielbasa, 139
Ribs, Instant Pot, 140–141
Rice
    Cilantro Lime Rice, 162
    One-Pot Creamy Sausage
        and Rice, 106
    Red Beans and Rice with
        Kielbasa, 139

S
Salads
    Cucumber Tomato Salad,
        145
    Easy Coleslaw, 143
    Fruit Salad, 148
    Grilled Vegetable Salad,
        158–159
    Simple Chopped Green
        Salad, 144
    Spinach Salad with
        Strawberries, 146–147
Salami, Charcuterie Board
    with, 56–57
Sandwiches and wraps
    Baked Brats with Onions
        and Peppers, 67
    BLT Sandwiches, 59

Carolina-Style BBQ
        Chicken Sandwiches,
        86–87
    Chili Cheese Dogs, 75
    Crispy Oven-Baked Wings,
        68–69
    Frozen Hamburgers Done
        Right, 72–73
    Grilled Chicken
        Quesadillas, 134–135
    Grilled Chicken Tender
        Sandwiches, 74
    Make-Ahead Breakfast
        Burritos, 28–29
    Make-Ahead Egg Muffin
        Sandwiches, 30–31
    Quick Philly Cheesesteak
        Sandwiches, 80–81
    Shredded Chicken Gyros,
        84–85
    Shredded Chicken Tacos,
        60–61
    Sloppy Joes, 62–63
    Turkey Lettuce Wraps, 66
Santa Fe Chicken Packets,
    122
Sauces to stock, 3
Sausage
    Baked Brats with Onions
        and Peppers, 67
    Baked Mostaccioli, 101
    Breakfast Scramble, 37
    Foil Packet Kielbasa with
        Potatoes and Peppers,
        118–119
    Make-Ahead Breakfast
        Burritos, 28–29
    Make-Ahead Breakfast
        "Quiche," 32–33
    Meatloaf Muffins, 93–95
    One-Pot Creamy Sausage
        and Rice, 106
    Red Beans and Rice with
        Kielbasa, 139
    Sausage Gravy and
        Biscuits, 42
    Spicy Andouille Sausage
        and Red Potatoes
        Packet, 116–117
    Tater Tot Breakfast
        Casserole, 48–49

Sheet Pan Chicken and
    Waffles, 46–47
Sheet Pan Chicken Tenders
    and Veggies, 110
Sheet Pan Steak Fajitas,
    108–109
Shepherd's Pie, Thanksgiving
    Style, 98–100
Shredded Chicken Gyros,
    84–85
Shredded Chicken Tacos,
    60–61
Shrimp, garlic butter, and
    peas, 125
Sides. See also Salads
    Cilantro Lime Rice, 162
    Foil Packet Broccoli on the
        Grill, 155
    Fresh Green Beans, 152
    Grilled Corn on the Cob,
        161
    Grilled Zucchini, 157
    Herbed Baby Potatoes, 151
    Ranch Beans, 149
    Summer Veggie Packet,
        153–154
Simple Chopped Green Salad,
    144
Skewers
    Beef and Tomato Skewers,
        79
    Best Beef Kebabs, 136–137
    Easy BBQ Meatball
        Skewers, 138
    Hawaiian Chicken
        Skewers, 71
Skillet Cake and Berries,
    166–167
Skillet dinner, Southwestern,
    103
Sloppy Joes, 62–63
S'mores Bake, 177
Snacks. See Lunch and
    snacks
Soup and chili
    Loaded Potato Soup, 82–83
    Stovetop Chili, 64–65
Southwestern Skillet Dinner,
    103
Spaghetti, one-pot, 107
Spices, 2

Spicy Andouille Sausage
    and Red Potatoes
    Packet, 116–117
Spinach
    Breakfast Frittata with, 45
    Spinach Salad with
        Strawberries, 146–147
    Summer Veggie Packet,
        153–154
Squash, sheet pan chicken
    tenders and, 110. See also
    Zucchini
Steak. See Beef
Storing food and water
    about: overview of
        considerations, 16–17
    cooler options and
        considerations, 19–21
    ice and, 18–19
    refrigerator/freezer
        considerations, 17–19
    water considerations,
        21–22
Stovetop Chili, 64–65
Stuffed Baked Potatoes,
    114–115
Summer Veggie Packet,
    153–154
Sweet and Sour Pork Packets,
    128–129
Sweet potatoes, in Shepherd's
    Pie, Thanksgiving Style,
    98–100

T
Tacos, shredded chicken,
    60–61
Tater Tot Breakfast Casserole,
    48–49
Thanksgiving-style shepherd's
    pie, 98–100
Toast (four toasting methods),
    26–27. See also French
    Toast
Tomatoes
    Beef and Tomato Skewers,
        79
    BLT Sandwiches, 59
    Caprese Chicken, 112–113
    pasta and (See Pasta)
    salads with (See Salads)

Turkey
    Shepherd's Pie,
        Thanksgiving Style,
        98–100
    Turkey Lettuce Wraps, 66

V
Vanilla Cream Steel Cut
    Oatmeal with Berries,
    51
Vegetables. See also Salads;
    specific vegetables
    Grilled Vegetable Salad,
        158–159
    Sheet Pan Chicken
        Tenders and Veggies, 110
    Summer Veggie Packet,
        153–154

W
Waffles, sheet pan chicken
    and, 46–47
Water considerations, 21–22
Watermelon, in Fruit Salad,
    148
Whiskey on the Rocks, 189
White Russian cocktail, hot,
    190

Y
Yogurt and Berry Parfait, 25
Yogurt, gyros with, 84–85

Z
Zucchini
    Grilled Vegetable Salad,
        158–159
    Grilled Zucchini, 157
    Summer Veggie Packet,
        153–154

Photo Credits